A Traveller's Wine Guide to
CALIFORNIA

A Traveller's Wine Guide to
CALIFORNIA

Text and photography
by Robert Holmes

Interlink Books

An imprint of Interlink Publishing Group, Inc.
Northampton, Massachusetts

First published in 2012 by
INTERLINK BOOKS
An imprint of
Interlink Publishing Group, Inc.
46 Crosby Street
Northampton
Massachusetts, 01060
www.interlinkbooks.com

Text copyright
© Philip Clark, 2012
Photography copyright
© Robert Holmes, 2012
Design copyright
© Interlink Publishing, 2012
Book design: James McDonald,
The Impress Group
Cover photo: Robert Holmes
Maps: Julian Ramirez

The Traveller's Wine Guides
series conceived by Philip Clark
Abbotsford, 14 Watts Road,
Tavistock, Devon
PL19 8LG, UK

Library of Congress
Cataloging-in-Publication Data
Holmes, Robert, 1943-
A traveller's wine guide to
California / by Robert Holmes.
    p. cm.
 Includes bibliographical references
and index.
 ISBN 978-1-56656-842-5 (pbk.)
1. Wine and wine making—Cali-
fornia. 2. Wineries—California.
I. Title. TP557.H65 2011
 641.2'209794--dc232011023568

Printed and bound in China

To request our complete 48-page
full-color catalog, please call us toll
free at 1-800-238-LINK, visit our
website at www.interlinkbooks.
com, or send us an e-mail:
info@interlinkbooks.com

Every effort has been made to
ensure accuracy, but the copyright
holder and publisher do not hold
themselves responsible for any
consequences that may arise from
errors or omissions. While the
content is believed to be correct at
the time of going to press, changes
may have occurred since that time,
or will occur during the currency
of the book.

ACKNOWLEDGMENTS

Writing this book has been a true
labor of love. I fell under the spell
of California's wine country soon
after moving there in 1979 and my
affair has continued with increasing
intensity.

   I have a multitude of people to
thank for welcoming me into their
world and giving me an education far
deeper than any academic institution
could manage. In particular Margrit
and the late Robert Mondavi, who
were always totally accessible; and I
must thank Margrit for the honor of
exhibiting my photographs at their
winery. Zelma Long, who taught me
how to taste wine many years ago.
Rob Davis for introducing me to the
legendary André Tchelistcheff.

   This book would not have been
possible without the support of
Philip Clark, who conceived the
Traveller's Wine Guide series. We
discussed the book for several years
before it became a reality.

   Last but in no way least, Andrea
Johnson for her constant, uncondi-
tional support and encouragement.
Her love of the wine industry is
unsurpassed.

For my daughters

Emma and Hannah Holmes

CONTENTS

How to use this book x

Introduction xii
The Winery Experience xiii
The System of Classification xiv
Traveling in California xvi
What to Drink xviii

Napa Valley 3
Napa Town 8
Yountville 10
Oakville and Rutherford 13
St Helena 20
Calistoga 25
The Silverado Trail 31
Los Carneros 42
Napa Valley—Where to stay and eat 49

Sonoma County 55
Santa Rosa 58
Sonoma Town 58
Sonoma Valley 62
Glen Ellen 63
Chalk Hill 65
Healdsburg 66
Alexander Valley 66
Dry Creek Valley 69
Russian River 71
Green Valley 73
Sonoma Coast 75
Sonoma County—Where to stay and eat 80

Mendocino County 83
Mendocino Town 83
Fort Bragg 86
Anderson Valley 86
Yorkville Highlands 88
Hopland 89
Redwood Valley 90
Lake County 94
Mendocino and Lake County—Where to stay and eat 98

San Francisco 101
Livermore 108

Santa Cruz Mountains... 111
San Francisco—Where to stay and eat................................ 116

Central Coast 119
Monterey County 122
Paso Robles 128
Edna Valley and Arroyo Grande 133
Central Coast—Where to stay and eat.................................. 138

Santa Barbara County 141
Santa Maria Valley 141
Santa Ynez Valley 146
Los Olivos 146
Santa Ynez Town 148
Solvang 149
Santa Rita Hills 150
Santa Barbara County—Where to stay and eat........................... 154

Southern California 157
Temecula 157
San Diego County 161
Los Angeles 161
Malibu 162
Southern California—Where to stay and eat 166

Central Valley 169
Lodi 172
Clarksburg 174
Madera 174
Central Valley—Where to stay and eat 179

Sierra Foothills 181
El Dorado County 184
Amador County 186
Calaveras County.. 190
Sierra Foothills—Where to stay and eat............................... 192

Beyond Wine 194
Brandy 194
Sake.. 196
Artisan foods 199

Websites 202
Wine events 203
Grape varieties 205
Further reading 208
Index 211

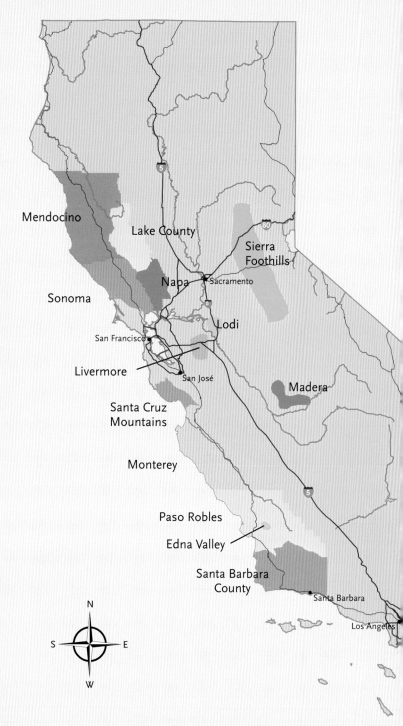

Mendocino

Lake County

Sierra
Foothills

Napa   ★ Sacramento

Sonoma

Lodi

San Francisco

Livermore   ● San José

Madera

Santa Cruz
Mountains

Monterey

Paso Robles

Edna Valley

Santa Barbara
County

Santa Barbara

Los Angeles

N
S ⊕ E
W

How to use this book

This book is designed for the visitor to California who not only wants to experience the wine country in all its diversity but also wants to explore the sites and attractions of California as a whole. Where else in the world can you experience a city like San Francisco, a 14,000-foot high mountain range, dramatic ocean scenery and Disneyland and still never be more than a couple of hours away from a winery? California has it all, including world-class wines, and our journey will include detours to some of the state's amazing attractions beyond the world of wine.

Wherever you travel in the state, vineyards will be somewhere on your route. The California wine industry is undoubtedly geared toward marketing and the majority of wineries encourage visitors and have facilities ranging from simple tasting rooms to full-scale retail outlets.

Most Californians buy their wine in supermarkets or specialist wine stores but many wineries offer wine for sale that is only available "at the cellar door" and these are usually small-production wines of only a few hundred cases. Most restaurants will allow you to bring your own wine, for a corkage fee, and this can be a very pleasant way to taste some of these scarce offerings.

Visiting wineries

You will find in this book names of local wine organizations that will be able to provide maps and lists of their member wineries. These can also be picked up at any winery you are visiting. Most of the regions also have a free weekly magazine that gives details of current events in the area. These too can be picked up at any winery.

The central theme of this book is about visiting wineries, but a number of wine-related events have been included that give the opportunity to taste sometimes hundreds of different wines in one place. A list of these events appears at the back of the book. As the better-known events are extremely popular, it's advisable to reserve tickets well before your planned visit.

Cabernet Sauvignon vines growing in Keyes Vineyard on Howell Mountain in Napa.

Touring wine country

This book is structured around the California highway system. It is the easiest, and cheapest, way to travel around the state, but not if you forget that the drinking and driving laws are extremely strict and rigorously enforced! The maps in this book are intended as a general guide and not to replace a detailed road atlas. The best source for maps is AAA (American Automobile Association), which has offices in most major towns. Not only are they excellent maps but they are free to members of AAA or overseas automobile associations such as the British AA.

California wine country is as varied as its wines. From the foothills of the Sierra Nevada mountains through the plains of the Sacramento River delta to the rolling hills of Sonoma and the fog of Santa Barbara County's Santa Rita hills, California offers a cornucopia of experiences.

INTRODUCTION

I F CALIFORNIA were an independent nation it would be the fourth leading wine-producing country in the world after Italy, France, and Spain.

Spanish missionaries introduced vines to California in the 1790s but it was not until the Gold Rush that winemaking became a commercial proposition. Hungarian Count Agoston Haraszthy established the first premium winery in Sonoma in 1857 and his Buena Vista Winery is still in operation today. Over the next two decades European immigrants built wineries throughout Napa, Sonoma, Santa Clara, and the Central Valley.

An outbreak of phylloxera, a tiny louse that feeds on the roots of vines, devastated most of the vineyards in the early 1900s, but the industry finally ground to a halt during the thirteen years of Prohibition; by 1933, when the law was repealed, the industry was in complete disarray. Only a handful of wineries were able to stay in business by making sacramental wines.

Techniques and rootstocks improved over the ensuing years to such an extent that by the early 1970s California wines could compete with the best in the world. When California wines won first place in a blind tasting in France (the celebrated 1976 "Judgment of Paris," see pages 25 and 34) competing against the finest French wines, California wine had truly arrived.

Today wine grapes are grown in 46 of California's 58 counties and account for over 90 percent of US wine production at 1,294 (and growing) commercial wineries. It would be ridiculous to suggest that all California wine is world class. Most of the wine made in California continues to be undistinguished jug wine from the Central Valley. The hot, dry climate is ideal for the robust grape varieties that make high-alcohol wines for a low price, but with little finesse. Fortunately small, boutique wineries are proliferating and the best are producing wines that are the equal of any in the world.

American Viticultural Areas

Unlike most wine-producing destinations, California has a vast range of *terroir* and the US Government has recognized 89 American Viticultural Areas (AVAs) in the state. This means that an enormous range of grape varieties are grown— over 33 red wine grapes and over 25 white wine grapes—and it's not unusual to find larger wineries producing ten or more different wines. Cabernet Sauvignon and Chardonnay still predominate, but production of lesser-known varieties such as Sangiovese and Viognier has increased tenfold over the past decade.

California's Central Valley is the breadbasket of the nation and although this region accounts for the biggest tonnage of grapes, few are made into good-quality wines. Most of the ultra-premium wine production is centered in Napa and Sonoma counties but remarkably good wines are also being made in other parts of the state, including Mendocino County, the Central Coast, Santa Ynez Valley, and even in the Sierra Nevada foothills. On a short visit to the state it's possible to experience a wide selection of the best California has to offer both in terms of wine, food, and sightseeing.

The winery experience

Visiting hours

Most tasting rooms are open seven days a week, usually from about 10AM to 4PM. Several tasting rooms in Napa County are only open by appointment because of strict local zoning laws, but a phone call from the gate is usually enough to get you in.

To spit or swallow?

Every tasting room will have a spittoon on the counter, although most people will use it to dump the remains in the glass. However, it is perfectly acceptable to spit into it and it's also highly recommended to do so. It's only too easy to consume large quantities of wine during a long day's tasting, which can seriously affect your critical judgment, not to mention your driving ability, and drunk driving in California is a very serious offense. Be very careful.

Tasting room etiquette

Tasting rooms never used to charge for tasting and it was always considered polite to purchase at least one bottle from the proprietor. Those days are gone, however, at least in Napa and Sonoma, and nearly every winery charges for tasting, some as much as $25. If you are paying to taste there is really no need to feel guilty if you don't buy wine. Usually you will be able to find the wines you are tasting in a local supermarket or discount wine store at a significantly lower price. However, some wines are only available at the winery and you may not have another opportunity to buy them.

Most wineries have a more modest $5 tasting fee, which often includes a souvenir wine glass, and it is only fair to support these wineries with direct purchases, especially as the tasting fee is usually deducted from the total.

The System of Classification

You would think good wine would be readily available throughout California, but don't be fooled. Many lower-priced, non-metropolitan restaurants will have only three wines on their list: Burgundy, Chablis, and Rosé. These will have as little in common with Burgundy and Chablis as Paris, Texas has with Paris, France. At their worst they can be obnoxious blends of low-quality fruit grown in the searing heat of California's Central Valley. The only redeeming factor is that all three are invariably served a few degrees above freezing, effectively masking their taste.

So how do you know what's in the bottle? Any wine with a generic name, such as Burgundy or Chablis, will almost certainly be unfit to drink unless you are really desperate. The fact that many are sold in cardboard cartons should also be an indication of quality to the astute imbiber. Beyond this point it gets more difficult and with luck this book will help negotiate the minefield.

RIDGE 2009
LYTTON SPRINGS®

71% ZINFANDEL, 23% PETITE SIRAH, 6% CARIGNANE
DRY CREEK VALLEY   14.5% ALCOHOL BY VOLUME
GROWN, PRODUCED & BOTTLED BY RIDGE VINEYARDS, INC.
650 LYTTON SPRINGS ROAD, HEALDSBURG, SONOMA COUNTY, CA 95448

The American Viticultural Area system

Most decent wine will be labeled with its AVA. This will tell you where the fruit was grown, but unlike European appellations it will give absolutely no indication about what the variety is or how the wine is made. It is purely a geographic demarcation. There is no control over yields, methods of vinification, or any of the other restrictions imposed by the controlled appellations of Europe. Vintners can do whatever they please with whatever fruit they choose and still label their wine with the AVA in which the fruit was grown or, more accurately, where at least 85 percent of the fruit was grown. A wine designated as a single vineyard must contain at least 95 percent of fruit from that vineyard. Vineyard land in California is now so expensive it would be foolhardy for anyone to produce anything less than the best wine of which they are capable.

Although the AVA system is relatively new, first introduced in 1978, several of the more prominent AVAs are now providing some guarantee of quality. Howell Mountain in Napa produces outstanding Cabernet Sauvignon and this has become the predominant grape grown here. Carneros, straddling the Napa/Sonoma border, produces excellent Chardonnay and Pinot Noir. Don't expect a delicate Pinot Noir from Amador County, where the hot summer temperatures are ideal for big Zinfandels and massive Rhône varieties. And don't expect big, high-alcohol Zinfandels from the cool vineyards of Russian River Valley.

Most wines will be labeled according to their variety—Merlot, Pinot Gris, Syrah, etc. At least 75 percent of the fruit must be from that variety and in the case of Cabernet Sauvignon, a small amount of Merlot or Cabernet Franc is often added to the blend to soften tannins.

Meritage wines

When a wine contains less than 75 percent of any single variety of grape, by law it has to be labeled as either a Red or White Table Wine. This generally applies to Bordeaux-style wines, which tend to be expensive. In 1988, to overcome the stigma of this generic labeling, the California wine industry coined the name Meritage, correctly pronounced like heritage, although more pretentious or ignorant establishments will pronounce the word with a long "a" as though it has a French origin. In order for a wine to be called a Meritage, the winery must belong to the Meritage Association, a marketing association with little control over quality. Many bottles simply labeled Red Table Wine are far superior to Meritage wines.

The very best way to assess the quality of a wine is to drink it, so let's start our journey through the Wine Country.

Traveling in California

The idea of traveling in California without a car is like mating with a gorilla. It is possible (or so I've been told), but is it worth the difficulty? Fortunately an excellent system of highways makes road travel painless. Freeways cross the state and, with speed limits of up to 70 mph, travel can be relatively fast. Unfortunately there is no lane discipline in California. Slow pokes will putter along in the fast lane so it's not surprising that people overtake on either side. Keep your eyes on your mirrors. Also keep your eyes open for commute lanes near cities. Cars with fewer than three passengers are prohibited from using these lanes during commute hours and violators are subject to very heavy fines. The lanes are always marked with diamond-shaped symbols and are well signed, giving detailed hours of operation. Travel during commute hours is always best avoided. Fuel, food, and accommodations are readily available and are well indicated at off-ramps.

Most of the major wine regions lie a short distance from Highway 101, which extends from Oregon to Los Angeles. This was the route pioneered by Father Junipero Serra while establishing missions throughout California over 200 years ago and it's not a coincidence that these missionaries established the first vineyards in California.

Napa and Sonoma

The most concentrated area of outstanding wineries is in the Napa Valley, a one-hour drive north of San Francisco. Highway 29 is the main route through the valley, but this two- and sometimes three-lane road is a nightmare on weekends, with a lethal combination of heavy tourist traffic and a surfeit of wine tasters.

Traffic on the rural backroads of Sonoma County is rarely congested. Although the county is no farther from San Francisco than Napa the wineries are far more low-key and spread over a much greater area. Perhaps the best way to visit the Napa and Sonoma wineries is on a personal tour offered by one of the many limousine services in San Francisco. Bus tours are also widely available if you don't mind group travel. After a day of wine tasting, having someone to drive you is not only more pleasant but safer.

Rail travel in California is

basic at best and no trains serve any of the wine-growing areas except for the **Wine Train**, which travels the short distance from the town of Napa to St Helena.

Hotels in the wine country tend to be small and expensive. Motels are a better deal but tend to be few and far between. Bed and breakfast inns are the preferred wine country accommodation, but these too come at a high premium. The popularity of these with both locals and tourists makes reservations difficult to get during the height of the season and advance planning is essential.

Driving in California is on the right and theoretically priority is on the right. Main roads always have priority. Roundabouts are very rarely encountered and most California drivers have no idea of how they should be negotiated. At stop lights, a right turn may be made on a red light if the road is clear but only after you have come to a complete halt.

Always carry a driver's license and evidence of insurance or the papers from the rental car company.

Seatbelts are mandatory in both the front and rear seats of the car and children weighing under 80 pounds may not travel in the front seat. Infants must be in children's safety seats.

It is illegal to use a cell-phone (mobile) when driving except with a headset.

Injury accidents must be reported to the local police or California Highway Patrol.

What to drink

Go into any store selling wine and every wine-filled shelf will be covered with labels, known in the trade as "shelf talkers," extolling the quality of different wines. They will often appear to be handwritten, but don't be deceived; they are just a marketing tool. The information given on these labels will be absolutely correct and accurate, but what does it mean?

Most often there will be a number ranging from 85 to 100. This is a scoring system developed by wine critic Robert Parker, and both the *Wine Spectator* and *Wine Enthusiast* magazines have adopted the same scale. The number will always be attributed to one of these sources and reflects their particular point of view—or taste.

Robert Parker has always been a fan of big, fruit-forward wines that often have high alcohol levels. He tends to give higher points to those wines than to delicate, elegant wines made in a more European style. The *Wine Spectator* leans in the same direction. If this parallels your personal taste then listen to what they recommend.

The highest possible score is 100 and is usually only given to the most expensive wines. These frequently increase in price after receiving the score and there has been harsh criticism of Parker et al. for having an insidious influence on the way wines are made. Any wine with a score in the 90s is considered very good but scores below 85 are rarely mentioned! An 84-point wine is usually universally disliked. However, it all comes down to personal taste.

Competitions

The other markers of quality are the medals won in winery competitions. There are a couple of things you should know about these. There are more and more competitions every year and they vary greatly in importance and quality of judging. Add to this the fact that wineries have to pay to enter and you can see that a gold medal is only meaningful if the competition has credibility and the entries from other wineries are of a high standard. Established wineries will often avoid wine competitions because they don't need the credibility conferred by medal counts.

The hierarchy of medals goes from Best of Show, Double Gold, Gold, Silver down to Bronze. The first three usually indicate a good, well-made wine, but the joke within the industry is that the wine has only to be wet to get a Bronze.

All of this, of course, is a question of taste. The answer is to take any of these recommendations lightly and develop your own palate by tasting as many wines as you can, determining your preferences. Some of the more reputable competitions include: California State Fair Commercial Wine Competition, Riverside International Wine Competition, and San Francisco Chronicle Wine Competition.

NAPA VALLEY

NAPA VALLEY IS THE BEGINNING and end of California wine country for most visitors. It is certainly the epicenter of the industry. The most famous—and expensive—cult wines are made here. It has the highest concentration of wineries and vineyards in the state and is an easy one-hour drive north of San Francisco. In addition, the compact size of the county—the distance between the towns of Napa in the south and Calistoga in the north is only 30 miles—makes it easy to cover in one day.

Charles Krug established the first commercial winery in the Valley in 1861 and by the end of the century there were over 140 wineries in operation. The wines being produced were no more than everyday table wines of little distinction and were intended for the local market. Then the phylloxera louse devastated most of the vineyards, which together with the enactment of Prohibition in 1920 virtually put an end to the wine trade.

The modern prominence of the Valley and its importance to the whole of the American wine industry has happened within the last 40 years. Robert Mondavi founded his eponymous winery in 1966. It was the first major winery to be built in the Valley since the Prohibition era. Mondavi set the standards for winemaking that would make California wines among the world's finest.

Although vineyards and wineries have been here since the mid-1800s, it was the legendary "Judgment of Paris" in 1976 that put Napa Valley wines on the world map. In this blind tasting of the best California and French wines the highest scores were given to a 1973 Chateau Montelena Chardonnay and a 1973 Stag's Leap Wine Cellars Cabernet Sauvignon, which beat the great Montrachets and Médocs of France.

Today, over 400 wineries are concentrated in the Valley and it appears that every square yard of cultivatable land is

« Harvesting Cabernet Sauvignon grapes at Bryant Family Vineyards on Pritchard Hill overlooking Lake Hennessey

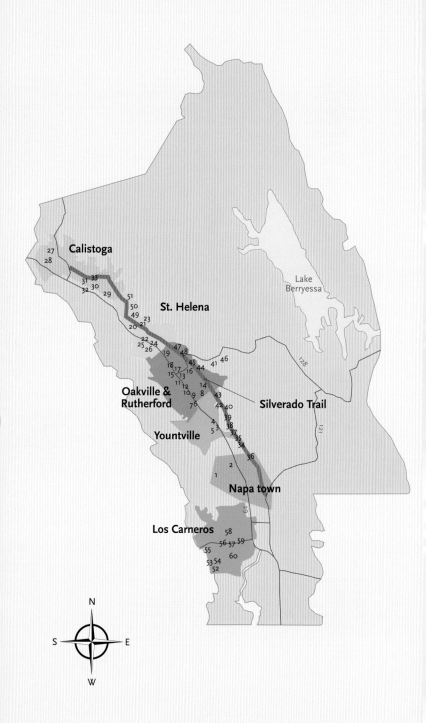

Napa Town

1. The Hess Collection
2. Trefethen Family Vineyards

Yountville

3. Somerston (Yountville Tasting Experience Center)
4. Vintage 1870
5. Domaine Chandon

Oakville and Rutherford

6. Cardinale Estate
7. Far Niente Winery
8. Silver Oak Winery
9. Robert Mondavi Winery
10. Turnbull Wine Cellars
11. St Supéry Vineyards and Winery
12. Cakebread Cellars
13. Peju Province Winery
14. Groth Vineyards & Winery
15. Rubicon Estate
16. Frog's Leap Winery
17. Beaulieu Vineyards
18. Grgich Hills Estate
19. Raymond Vineyards

St Helena

20. Spring Mountain Vineyard
21. Beringer Vineyards
22. Heitz Wine Cellar
23. Charles Krug Winery
24. V Sattui Winery
25. Hall Wines St Helena
26. The Room, Flora Springs Winery

Calistoga

27. Chateau Montelena Winery
28. Summers Estate Wines
29. Schramsberg Vineyards
30. Sterling Vineyards
31. Clos Pegase
32. Twomey Cellars
33. Cuvaison Estate Wines

The Silverado Trail

34. Clos du Val
35. Chimney Rock
36. Darioush
37. Stag's Leap Cellars
38. Pine Ridge Winery
39. Silverado Vineyards
40. Robert Sinskey Winery
41. Somerston Vineyards
42. Cliff Lede Winery
43. Paraduxx Winery
44. ZD Wines
45. Mumm Napa Valley
46. Kuleto Estate Winery
47. Quintessa
48. Rutherford Hill Winery
49. Duckhorn Vineyards
50. Rombauer Vineyards
51. Failla

Los Carneros

52. Viansa Winery & Vineyards
53. Cline Cellars
54. Jacuzzi Family Vineyards
55. Gloria Ferrer Caves & Vineyard
56. Domaine Carneros
57. Cuvaison
58. Artesa Vineyards & Winery
59. Saintsbury
60. Bouchaine Vineyards

A tasting room in Napa. When sampling wines, it helps to avoid wearing perfume or aftershave as these can interfere with the aroma

planted with vines. There are 45,000 acres of vineyards in the county and from the town of Napa all the way up to Calistoga and beyond, vineyards cover the Valley floor and stretch beyond into the surrounding hillsides, where some of the finest Cabernet Sauvignon fruit is grown. The steep hillsides of the Mayacamas Mountains to the west and the Vaca Mountains to the east offer **terroir** that creates fruit with amazing intensity and depth. With the international success of Napa

wines, winery ownership has become a status symbol for new-found wealth, and money has flooded into the Valley creating an air of opulence and excess that at times reaches Disneyesque proportions. Ironically, Napa Valley is second only to Disneyland as a tourist attraction.

For the visitor, the downside to this success is traffic. During summer weekends until the end of harvest in October, **Highway 29**, the main road through Napa and St Helena to Calistoga, can become a parking lot. Midweek is the best time to visit Napa Valley and if you must go at the weekend, use the Silverado Trail (see page 31), which avoids the main towns.

Napa grape varieties

The most notable wine of Napa is Cabernet Sauvignon, with over 18,200 acres planted. It is usually made as a single varietal but occasionally blended with Merlot, Cabernet Franc or Petite Verdot to create a classic Bordeaux-style blend. The most expensive Napa Cabernets are usually big, bold, fruit-forward, high-alcohol wines with strong overtones of chocolate, cherry, mint and cedar.

Second only to Cabernet Sauvignon is Chardonnay, with 7,300 acres planted. More than 30 different soil types have been identified in Napa County. Combined with microclimates ranging from the warm northern end of the Valley near Calistoga to the Los Carneros region where the influence of the San Pablo Bay cools down the nights, a wide range of varietals are able to thrive including Merlot, Syrah, Zinfandel, Pinot Noir, Sauvignon Blanc, Viognier, Cabernet Franc and Sémillon, but Cabernet remains king.

Napa County produces about 5 percent of all California wine. Napa has

A block of Chimney Rock's Cabernet Sauvignon vines in the Stags Leap district. Chimney Rock makes wines from grapes grown on its own

something to offer for everyone and is well worth a visit if only for a voyeuristic experience of the "good life."

Napa Town

While Napa Valley has all the glamour and glitz of Hollywood, the town of Napa at the southern end of the Valley has always been a blue-collar enclave. Well over half the population of Napa County lives here and, at almost 80,000 people, this is the biggest town in the Valley. Napa sits on the bank of the Napa River and historically the town was an important port. Small cruise ships still stop here on their meanderings up the Sacramento Delta. What the town lacked in charm was more than compensated by low property prices. But this situation is rapidly changing. Property prices are no longer the bargain they once appeared and recent urban renewal projects including a dramatic revitalization of the riverfront have transformed Napa into an attractive destination that is still looking for its soul but is well on its way to finding it.

Copia

The transformation was given a kick-start with the building of COPIA: The American Center for Food, Wine and the Arts. This ambitious museum, art gallery, theater and restaurant complex struggled to find its identity and sadly closed its doors in 2009. The center was the dream of the late Robert Mondavi, who was a major donor, and it was arguably the start of his philanthropic gestures that led to the fall of the House of Mondavi. At the time of writing, the building stands empty, waiting for an appropriate occupant, and is the source of great debate within the Napa community. Next door to the COPIA building, **Oxbow Public Market** delivers a 40,000 square foot covered market filled with artisan food and wine and several prepared food outlets. This is an ideal place to get an inexpensive snack or even a more substantial meal in very casual surroundings. The gentrification of Napa has attracted several exceptionally good restaurants to town, including Michelin-starred **Ubuntu** that serves exclusively vegetarian food

Napa's famous Wine Train stops at Grgich Hills Estate in Rutherford during its four-hour journey

in a building shared with a yoga studio.

Beautifully restored Victorian houses line the quiet tree-lined streets of Napa but the architectural jewel is the town's **Napa Valley Opera House**. Built in 1879, it is one of California's last second-story theaters. After being closed for 88 years, the building was painstakingly restored and returned to the community for its original purpose—entertainment.

The wine train

Many visitors come to Napa to board the Wine Train, which departs twice daily from Napa to St Helena in the heart of the Valley for a four-hour journey including lunch or dinner. Although the train was initially a matter of great controversy it is now an established part of the Napa landscape and several wineries once opposed to its intrusion into the rural landscape now welcome the wine-buying visitors with open arms.

There are no wineries in town but one must-see winery can only be approached through Napa on a 15-minute drive up Mont Veeder from Highway 29. **The Hess Collection** is owned by Swiss mineral water magnate Donald Hess who leased the old, stone Mont LaSalle Cellars and added to the winery two floors of world-class contemporary art including work by Robert Motherwell, Francis Bacon and Frank Stella. The winery's Cabernet and Chardonnays can be sampled in the ground-floor tasting room.

Just to the north of town, right off Highway 29, is one of the great historic wineries of the Valley. **Trefethen Vineyards** occupies an old winery built in 1886 and it is the last wooden, three-storey gravity-flow winery in California. A horse-drawn winch pulled grapes up to the third floor for the crush and gravity carried the juice to the second floor for fermentation and down to the first floor for barrel aging. A tour is recommended if only to see the vast barrel room. The wines are all made with estate fruit from the surrounding vineyards and the reserve wines are particularly notable.

WINERIES & MORE

The Hess Collection
4411 Redwood Road
Napa, CA 94558

Tel: 707 255 1144
www.hesscollection.com
Open daily 10AM–5:30PM.
for self-guided tours.
Private tours by
reservation only.

Trefethen Family Vineyards
1160 Oak Knoll Avenue
Napa, CA 94558
Tel: 707 255 7700
www.trefethen.com
Open daily 10AM–4:30PM.

ATTRACTIONS
Valley Wine Train
1275 McKinstry Street
Napa, CA 94559
Tel: 707 253 2111
www.winetrain.com
Daily at 10:30AM
and 5:30PM.

Napa Valley Opera House
1030 Main Street
Napa, CA 94559
Tel: 707 226 7372
www.nvoh.org

Yountville

Once you leave Napa, going north on Highway 12, vineyards dominate the landscape. George Yount, the first American to settle in Napa Valley, planted the first of these vines over 150 years ago. He established Sebastopol (not to be confused with the present-day Sebastopol in neighboring Sonoma County) in the heart of the Valley as the result of a land grant from the Mexican government and in 1867, after Yount's death, the name was changed to Yountville in his honor.

Until fairly recently Yountville was a quiet dormitory town for winery workers but all that changed in the early 1990s when Thomas Keller arrived and turned **The French Laundry** into one of the great restaurants of the world. Other establishments followed over the next few years, and today there are no fewer than four Michelin-starred restaurants within a quarter of a mile of each other, including the three-star French Laundry, considered by many to be the best restaurant in America. Reservations must be made two months in advance and they are the hottest ticket in town.

Yountville has become a gourmet mecca with one restaurant for every 400 residents, and along with the restaurants came boutique hotels and fine shopping. **Vintage 1870**, housed in a multi-story brick building, was originally the Groezinger Winery. Now it is full of trendy boutiques, galleries and **Bottega**, a restaurant owned by celebrity chef Michel Chiarello that has become a magnet for the rich and famous.

Somerston Estate has opened a wonderful destination tasting room opposite the **Villagio Inn and Spa** on Washington Street. Their winery and vineyards are several miles away, high above the Valley on the way to Lake Berryessa. The only winery in town is across Highway 29.

Domaine Chandon is the California outpost of Champagne's Moët & Chandon and, like its European parent, concentrates on sparkling wines. The winery is set in park-like grounds and it is one of the only wineries in the Valley to house its own award-winning restaurant, **Etoile**, serving lunch and dinner every day. A short distance up the road from Domaine Chandon, the **Napa Valley Museum** is worth a visit if only to see the permanent exhibition: **California Wine: The Science of an Art**. This could serve as a model for all museums with its lively, fun exhibits.

For a different perspective on the Valley, Yountville is the perfect place to hop into a balloon and float above the vineyards. Most mornings, before dawn, the roar of propane burners breaks the silence as the massive canopies of hot-air balloons are inflated, ready for take-off. The flight will end with a champagne brunch in celebration of perhaps the most perfect way to experience Napa Valley.

WINERIES & MORE

Somerston
6488 Washington Street
Yountville, CA 94599
Tel: 707 967 8414
www.somerstonwineco.com
Open daily 10AM–10PM

Vintage 1870
6525 Washington Street
Yountville, CA 94599
Tel: 707 944 2451
www.vmarketplace.com
Open daily 10AM–5:30PM.

Sunrise lights up the post-harvest vines at the Somerston Estate vineyards high above Lake Hennessey

Domaine Chandon
1 California Drive
Yountville, CA 94599
Tel: 707 944 2280
www.chandon.com
Winery open daily
10AM–6PM.

Etoile Restaurant
Tel: 800 736 2892
Restaurant open
Thurs-Mon 11:30AM–
2:30PM and 6PM–9:30PM.

ATTRACTIONS
Napa Valley Museum
55 Presidents Circle
Yountville, CA 94599

Tel: 707 944 0500
www.napavalleymuseum.org
Open 10AM–5PM. Closed
Tues and major holidays.

Oakville and Rutherford

You could pass Oakville
and Rutherford without
even realizing that they ex-
ist, but the most expensive
vineyard land in Califor-
nia, in fact in all of North
America, is within a few
square miles of these twin
settlements. Not that any
land is available for sale.

Every inch is planted with vines, mostly Cabernet Sauvignon, that produce some of the most sought-after wines in the country. If Napa Valley is the epicenter of the California wine industry, this is the epicenter of Napa. Here you will find the Valley's greatest concentration of premium wineries, but there is little else of interest apart from the **Oakville Grocery**, a Napa tradition offering delectable gourmet items for the perfect picnic.

Oakville

High on a knoll, just before you enter Oakville, **Cardinale Winery** offers sweeping views of its estate vineyards set to a backdrop of Mount St Helena. One wine is made here, a massive, blockbuster Cabernet Sauvignon with the Cardinale label. The winery is one of the jewels in the crown of the Jess Jackson empire, whose Kendall-Jackson brand is one of the most recognized in America.

Oakville Grade Road climbs steeply over Mount Veeder and eventually descends into Sonoma Valley.

Before the road starts its tortuous climb, **Far Niente Winery** can be seen to the left, partially hidden by trees. The building dates back to 1885, was abandoned in 1919 at the onset of Prohibition and inevitably fell into disrepair. In 1979, Gil Nikel, a nurseryman from Oklahoma—his family's nursery happens to be the second biggest in the USA—bought the derelict building, completely restored it to its original condition and planted gardens worthy of a nurseryman. The building is now on the National Register of Historic Places. The winery and gardens are worth visiting in their own right but add to that a collection of historic cars and the wine almost becomes an afterthought. But it shouldn't. Far Niente makes only three wines and each one is exquisite. Cabernet Sauvignon, Chardonnay and Dolce (a late-harvest Sémillon and Sauvignon Blanc blend—think Yquem) represent some of the best wine coming out of Napa. Far Niente visits are strictly by appointment.

Turn back onto Highway 29 and immediately turn right onto Oakville Cross

Peter Mondavi, brother of Robert, is one of the last pioneers of the Napa wine industry still working, well into his nineties

Road to visit **Silver Oak Winery**. The winery was recently rebuilt after a devastating fire but their big Cabernet Sauvignons aged exclusively in American oak continue to be as popular as ever. A sister winery has been opened in Alexander Valley surrounded by vineyards that provide the fruit for their Alexander Valley Cabernet.

The Mondavi winery

Opposite Oakville Grocery, a distinctive bell tower marks the most celebrated winery in the Valley. The Mondavi family story is true soap opera material. Robert Mondavi started his eponymous winery after a family feud with his brother Peter at the historic Charles Krug winery a few miles up the road. Robert's dream was to create a cutting-edge winery that would be inherited by his children in the tradition of the great European wine family dynasties. Although the winery was established only in 1966 it rapidly became the flagship for California

Beaulieu Vineyards' legendary George Latour Cabernet Sauvignon is poured in the reserve tasting room at the company's Rutherford winery

winemaking and Mondavi's influence has had a pivotal effect on California's wine industry. In keeping with his visionary thinking, he partnered with Baron Philippe de Rothschild to produce Opus One, a Bordeaux-style wine that was the most expensive in North America when it was first produced. **The Opus One** winery is the architectural masterpiece—or disaster, depending on your viewpoint—directly across Highway 12. Within a few years, family feuds, repeating the pattern of the previous generation, led to the collapse of the empire and the **Robert Mondavi Winery** is now owned and operated by Constellation Brands, the world's biggest wine conglomerate.

A little further north, **Turnbull Cellars** mounts revolving photographic exhibits from the owner's formidable collection. This is museum-quality work and worth viewing in its own right.

Another destination winery with revolving art exhibits is just a little further north. **St Supéry's** wines may not have the cachet of some of their famous neighbors but the **Wine Discovery Center** and the self-guided winery tour are among the best in the Valley. A display vineyard demonstrates different methods of pruning and trellising along with examples of the main varietals growing in the Valley. The "smell-a-vision" exhibit alone, where you can actually smell the components of red and white wines, makes the visit worthwhile.

Other significant wineries in Oakville include **Cakebread Cellars**, **Peju Province** and **Groth**.

Rutherford

The Rutherford Bench is the source of some of the best Cabernet Sauvignon fruit in the state and it shouldn't be surprising that many iconic wineries are concentrated here.

Turn off Highway 29 onto Niebaum Lane and drive down a tree-lined avenue to one of the grand old wineries of California. The old Inglenook Estate was founded in 1879 by a sea captain, Gustave Neibaum. Francis Ford Coppola, the film director, renamed it **Rubicon Estate** and now owns the magnificent ivy-covered building and surrounding vineyards. Winery tours include exhibits of memorabilia from many of Coppola's films including Don Corleone's desk and chair from *The Godfather* and a museum-quality collection of antique Zoetropes and magic lanterns.

Frog's Leap is just a short detour down Rutherford Cross Road. John Williams, an ex-dairy farmer from upstate New York, established Frog's Leap as a brand in 1981 and moved into the present location in 1994. The winery is housed in the Red Barn, the oldest board-and-batten building in Napa Valley. Williams has always believed in ecologically sound practices using recycled materials and solar energy, and his was the first organically certified vineyard in Napa Valley as long ago as 1987. The high quality of the wines, particularly Cabernet Sauvignon and Sauvignon Blanc, belie the sense of humor and relaxed approach to wine promoted at Frog's Leap, whose motto is "Time's Fun When You're Having Flies."

One of the oldest wineries in Napa occupies a vine-covered building right on Highway 29 at Rutherford Cross. Georges de Latour

17

established **Beaulieu Vineyards** in 1900 and it is one of the few wineries that weathered Prohibition and kept the doors open by switching their focus to sacramental wines. During this period de Latour had continued to make Cabernet Sauvignon and patiently let it age in the cellars until Prohibition ended in 1933 when Beaulieu wines were ready to be released to a thirsty public. De Latour realized that if he was to make wines to match the finest in France he needed European talent and in 1938 persuaded the legendary Andre Tchelistcheff to move from Paris to Rutherford. The rest is history. Tchelistcheff was to change the face of California winemaking. He was not only the architect of Georges de Latour Private Reserve, still a benchmark Cabernet Sauvignon, but he went on to consult across the industry and raised the level of winemaking to truly world-class standards.

A little further north on Highway 29 is the unimposing building of **Grgich Hills Estate**. Mike Grgich has been making wine in Napa Valley for over 50 years and his most celebrated achievement was the crafting of a Chardonnay for Chateau Montelena that beat the very best wines from France in the 1976 "Judgment of Paris." Grgich was responsible for introducing many breakthrough winemaking techniques, including malolactic fermentation and the use of oak barrels for proper aging. He was also a long-time proponent of organic farming and sustainable vineyard practices long before it became fashionable.

Zinfandel Lane forms the northern border of the Rutherford AVA. Turn right off Highway 29 and **Raymond Vineyards'** driveway is a short distance down on the right. Roy Raymond established the 90-acre estate in 1971 after working with the Beringers for 35 years. He married Martha Beringer in 1936. The Raymond wines were good but after the winery was sold to the Japanese several years ago the brand languished. In August 2009 the property became part of the Boisset Family Estates empire. Jean-Charles Boisset has ambitious plans to make the winery a showplace for biodynamic farming. All the estate vineyards will eventually be certified organic like Boisset's sister property, DeLoach in Sonoma's Russian River Valley. Raymond is a winery to watch.

WINERIES & MORE

Cardinalwate
7600 St Helena Highway
Oakville, CA 94562
Tel: 707 948 2643
www.cardinale.com
Open daily by appointment only 10:30AM–5PM.

Far Niente Winery
1350 Acacia Drive
Napa, CA 94558
Tel: 707 944 2861
www.farniente.com
Open daily by appointment 10AM–4PM.

Silver Oak Winery
915 Oakville Crossroad
Oakville, CA 94562
Tel: 707 942 7022
www.silveroak.com
Open Mon–Sat 9AM–5PM.
Reservations required for groups and tours.

Robert Mondavi Winery
7801 St Helena Highway
Oakville, CA 94562
Tel: 707 226 1395
www.robertmondaviwinery.com
Open daily 10AM–5PM.

Turnbull Wine Cellars
8210 St Helena Highway
Oakville, CA 94562
Tel: 800 887 6285
www.turnbullwines.com
Open daily 10AM–4PM.

St Supéry Vineyards and Winery
8440 St Helena Highway
Rutherford, CA 94573
Tel: 707 963 4507
www.stsupery.com
Open daily 10AM–5PM except major holidays.

Cakebread Cellars
8300 St Helena Highway
Rutherford, CA 94573
Tel: 800 588 0298
www.cakebread.com
Open by appointment only 10AM–4PM.

Peju Province Winery
8466 St Helena Highway
Rutherford, CA 94573
Tel: 800 446 7358
www.peju.com
Open daily 10AM–6PM.
Closed Thanksgiving, Christmas Day.

Groth Vineyards & Winery
750 Oakville Cross Road
Oakville, CA 94562
Tel: 707 754 4254
www.grothwines.com
Open by appointment only Mon–Sat 10AM–4PM.

Rubicon Estate
1991 St Helena Highway
Rutherford, CA 94573
Tel: 707 968 1100
www.rubiconestate.com
Open daily 10AM–5PM.

Frog's Leap Winery
8815 Conn Creek Road
Rutherford, CA 94573
Tel: 707 963 4704
www.frogsleap.com
Open Mon–Sat 10AM–4PM.

Beaulieu Vineyards
1960 St Helena Highway
Rutherford, CA 94573
Tel: 707 967 5233
www.bvwines.com
Open daily 10AM–5PM
except major holidays.

Grgich Hills Estate
1829 St Helena Highway
Rutherford, CA 94573
Tel: 707 963 2784
www.grgich.com
Open daily 9:30AM–4:30PM
except major holidays.

Raymond Vineyards
849 Zinfandel Lane
St Helena, CA 94574
Tel: 800 525 2659
www.raymondvineyards.com
Open daily 10AM–4PM.

St Helena

St Helena is at the heart of
Napa Valley both geo-
graphically and as a center
for tourist activity. Henry
Still built a store here in
1854 and gave away build-
ing lots to anyone wanting
to start a business. Within
a few years a community
developed and by 1858 a
Dr Crane planted a vine-
yard that would be the first
to produce wine commer-
cially in Napa. Charles
Krug established his eponymous winery a couple of
years later and more soon
followed.

Physically the town hasn't
changed very much over
the last 150 years. Gone are
most of the small-town
shops, replaced by high-
end boutiques and galleries
catering to the throngs of
tourists clogging Highway
29 through the center of
town. The old, weathered
stone and brick buildings
remain relatively un-
changed, however. St Helena is small and a short walk
a couple of blocks off Main
Street (Highway 29) into
the residential areas gives
a feel of the town as it was
before wine became king.
The local library houses a
**Robert Louis Stevenson
Museum** that celebrates
the author's sojourn in St
Helena when he wrote *The
Silverado Squatters*.

Greystone, the former Christian Brothers winery, is now home to the Napa headquarters of the Culinary Institute of America

Some of the Valley's best restaurants are located here as well as a handful of wineries, including **Sutter Home Winery**, which "invented" the white Zinfandel that rapidly became one of California's best-selling wines. So much for the popular palate of North America! A short distance from town, **Spring Mountain Winery** is a Victorian gem set in wonderful landscaped gardens. The building was used as the iconic Napa winery in the 1980s television series *Falcon Crest*. Tastings of their very limited production Bordeaux blends and Cabernet Sauvignon are given by appointment only in the splendid dining room of Miravalle, the beautiful Victorian house designed by Albert Schropfer, who was also the architect of Beringer's Rhine House.

Just north of town **Beringer** is one of the grand old wineries of California and the recently restored **Rhine House** one of the great architectural masterpieces of Napa Valley. The winery has passed through a series of hands and is currently owned by Fosters, of Australian lager fame. The wines of Beringer cover the gamut of tastes from white Zinfandel to outstanding Cabernet Sauvignons crafted by their former winemaker Ed Sbragia, one of the great winemakers of California.

The Culinary Institute of America

Continue out of town on Highway 29 and on the left is the massive stone building of **Greystone Cellars** that was formerly the home of the Christian Brothers, a monastic group making brandy that is still marketed under their name. The stone building was constructed from volcanic rock that came from the extinct volcano Mount St Helena. Today Greystone is the home of the western outpost of the Culinary Institute of America, the foremost culinary school in the country. A small museum of food and wine is open to the public along with the **Campus Store** and **Spice Islands Market**. A wide selection of cookbooks and kitchen tools as well as regular cooking classes and demonstrations will make the visit worthwhile for anyone with a culinary interest. Their dining room is also open

The Rhine House at Beringer Vineyards dates back to 1884. A quarter of the original construction costs went to 40 stained glass windows

to the public and although you will be fed by students, these are some of the best and most accomplished culinary professionals in the world.

Opposite Greystone is another building on the National Register of Historical Landmarks. **Charles Krug Winery** was established in 1861 and it is the oldest surviving winery in California. Cesare Mondavi, together with his sons Peter and Robert, restored the winery in 1943 but Robert left in the 1960s to start a winery in Oakville after an acrimonious family feud. Charles Krug is still run by Peter and his sons.

South of St Helena a handful of wineries are worthy of attention. Within a city block of each other are one of the largest and the smallest.

V Sattui Winery is a big tourist attraction. The impressive 1885 building is operated by the fourth generation of Sattuis in the wine business. It is the only winery in the Valley with a deli, making it a very popular picnic stop, but you must buy your fare at the winery's deli. Fortunately it is very well stocked. You may never have tasted, or even heard of, Sattui wine because it is sold exclusively at the winery and almost 50 different wines are produced. Dario Sattui is now at the helm. A few miles north of St Helena he recently completed one of Napa's biggest attractions, popularly known as **Sattui Castle**, although Dario named it Castello di Amorosa. This medieval Tuscan castle is a Las Vegas-meets-Disneyland experience and it is mercifully hidden from Highway 29. Just as white Zinfandel is hugely popular, so is Sattui's castle!

Joe Heitz has made some of the most respected Cabernet Sauvignon in Napa. He was right-hand man to the legendary Andre Tchelistcheff at Beaulieu Vineyard and went on to launch the highly respected Department of Enology at Fresno State University. In 1961, with his wife Alice, he purchased eight acres of vineyard land south of St Helena and set the course to put **Heitz Cellars** on the map of every serious wine enthusiast. His Martha's Vineyard Cabernet is outstanding, with unique notes of eucalyptus and mint. The tasting room is a small, unpretentious one-room building and certainly doesn't reflect the importance of the wines. Heitz may be legendary for its Cabernets but ask to taste the port. This is one of the few California wineries to make a truly authentic-tasting port using traditional Portuguese varietals.

Directly opposite Heitz, and you have to play Russian Roulette to cross Highway 29 to get from one to the other, **Hall Wines** is an extensive development fronted by a small tasting room pouring a selection of impressive red wines from their estate vineyards. Entrepreneurs Craig and Kathryn Hall own the winery, and the winemaking facilities to the rear are used by several prominent Napa wineries. It is a well-established custom crush facility. A massive rebuilding program is underway with a central building that is the first winery project by renowned architect **Frank Gehry**. It has been the subject of great debate within the community with many residents considering the futuristic design totally incongruous. The Halls have another property in

Rutherford that is open by appointment only and it houses some of Craig Hall's extensive art collection.

Flora Springs Winery and Vineyard is a third-generation family winery set in the foothills of the Mayacamus Mountains just outside St Helena. Visits to the winery and cave are available by appointment but a new tasting room has recently been opened on Highway 29 next to **Dean and DeLuca**, the well-known epicurean market owned by Leslie Rudd of Rudd Vineyards. It is a difficult building to miss. The Gaudiesque exterior and interior are a startling contrast to anything nearby but the wines are far better than the Toontown atmosphere would suggest. The Cabernet Sauvignon in particular is extremely good as is Trilogy, a classic Bordeaux blend.

WINERIES & MORE

Spring Mountain Vineyard
2805 Spring Mountain Road
St Helena, CA 94574-1798
Tel: 707 967 4188
www.springmountainvineyard.com
Open by appointment only.

Beringer Vineyards
2000 Main Street
St Helena, CA 94574
Tel: 707 967 4412
www.beringer.com
Open May 29–Oct 22
10AM–6PM, Oct 23–May 28
10AM–5PM.

Heitz Wine Cellar
436 St Helena
Highway South
St Helena, CA 94574-2206
Tel: 707 963 3542
www.heitzcellar.com
Open daily 11AM–4:30PM
except major holidays.

Charles Krug Winery
2800 Main Street
St Helena, CA 94574
Tel: 707 967 2200
www.charleskrug.com
Open daily 10:30AM–5PM
except major holidays.

V Sattui Winery
1111 White Lane
St Helena, CA 94574-1599
Tel: 707 963 7774
www.vsattui.com
Open daily 9AM–6PM
(9AM–5PM in winter).
Closed Christmas Day.

Hall Wines St Helena
401 St Helena
Highway South
St Helena, CA 94574
Tel: 707 967 2626
Open daily 10AM–5:30PM.

**The Room,
Flora Springs Winery**
677 South St
Helena Highway
St Helena, CA 94574
Tel: 707 967 8032/
　　866 967 8032
www.florasprings.com
Open daily 10:30AM–5PM.

Calistoga

The glitz of Napa Valley
fades toward its northern
end, but this has nothing
to do with the quality of
the wine produced here.
After all, this is the home
of **Chateau Montelena
Winery**, which produced
the legendary Chardonnay
that won the Judgment of
Paris tasting in 1976.

　Calistoga sits close to the
extinct volcano Mount St
Helena. Here, in the Old
West atmosphere of the
main street, the upscale
boutiques of nearby St
Helena are noticeably
absent. Replacing high-end
wine merchants selling
exclusive and outrageously
expensive bottles of local
cult wines, Calistoga is
home to the **Wine Garage**,
where no wine costs over
$25 and the owner searches
for small vintners making
undervalued wines.
Calistoga is that kind of

place—less pretentious and far more real than St Helena and Yountville a few miles to the south. It is the ideal base for those wanting to avoid crowds and high prices.

Volcanic activity is the soul of Calistoga, from tacky tourist attractions such as **Old Faithful of California Geyser**—one of only three in the world to erupt with precise regularity—to the mineral springs and mud baths of over a dozen spas. These are the perfect places to relax after a hard day's wine tasting but don't expect a lot of glitz. Most of the spas and hot springs are far from glamorous but they give visitors a cost-effective way of experiencing the healing waters and mud baths of Napa Valley.

California's first millionaire, Samuel Brannan, recognized the potential of Calistoga as a health resort in the mid-1800s and it was Brannan who gave the town its name, a combination of California and Saratoga Springs, a famous resort in upstate New York.

Calistoga's wineries

Wineries soon followed the health spas but it wasn't until 2010 that Calistoga was granted its own AVA designation. Perhaps this lack of recognition was the reason that this part of the Valley has always been in the shadow of more famous appellations to the south. This northern end of the Valley has hot summer days and cool nights but it's far enough away from the San Pablo Bay and the Pacific coast to be unaffected by their moderating influence. Combined with the volcanic soils of the region, this is the perfect terroir for big red wines such as Cabernet Sauvignon and Zinfandel.

Chateau Montelena is a short distance east of the Old Faithful Geyser. The winery was built in 1882 and in the early 1950s was sold to a Chinese engineer who built a five-acre lake with three islands connected by Chinese-style bridges. The Barrett family bought the property in 1972, replanted the

Early-morning sun streams through the smoke-filled Demptos cooperage. A French-owned company, Demptos opened its Napa subsidiary in 1982

vineyards, restored the winery buildings and hired Mike Grgich as winemaker. It was the winery's second release of Chardonnay that won the Judgment of Paris tasting. Recently, the winery and Barrett family were the subjects of the movie *Bottle Shock*.

Summers Estate Winery is a new kid on the block and if you really must see Old Faithful erupt you can get a good, and free, view from the winery's picnic area. Jim and Beth Summers have a love affair with Charbono, which is little grown outside California and with only 80 acres under vine in the whole state. Forty of those acres are in Calistoga. A visit to Summers Estate gives a very rare opportunity to taste this big, red wine.

Almost directly across the road from Old Faithful is one of the great sights of the wine country. In 1987 Italian artist Carlo Marchiori bought five acres of land on which he built **Villa Ca'Toga** in homage to Italian culture. The rooms are masterpieces of **trompe l'oeil** art and the grounds are full of credibly realistic Greco-Roman ruins, Thai stupas and a Roman pool.

Tours of the house, which is Marchiori's home, are only available on Saturday mornings during the summer. Otherwise visit Marchiori's art gallery just off Calistoga's main street.

South of Calistoga but still within the new Calistoga AVA are three must-see wineries. **Schramsberg Vineyards** is one of the oldest wineries in Napa Valley, founded by Jacob Schram in 1862. By 1965 the place was in ruins but Jack and Jamie Davies came along and completely restored the buildings and gardens to their original glory. They also set the course that made Schramsberg a leader in producing outstanding sparkling wines by the *méthode champenoise*. Schramsberg was one of the first wineries in the area to use the traditional champagne blends of Chardonnay and Pinot Noir for their wines. In the early 1960s very few of these varietals had been planted in Napa Valley.

Sterling Vineyards is one of the more visually prominent wineries in the Valley with its white, monastic-looking building sitting on a hilltop high above the vineyards. The winery has been through a succession of ownerships and is now part of the massive UK drinks conglomerate Diageo. Like many large wineries, the list of wines it produces is huge with 18 varieties and even more single vineyard bottlings. The wines are generally very well made but the real attraction of Sterling for many visitors is the **aerial tram** that provides the only way up to the winery from the parking lot below. The ride is worthwhile if only for the view down the Valley.

Across the road from Sterling is one of the better examples of new architecture in Napa. The eminent post-modernist architect Michael Graves designed **Clos Pegase** as a temple to wine and art for owner Jan Schrem, who made his fortune in publishing in Japan. The winery is home to Schrem's outstanding art collection and one of the highlights of a visit is an audio-visual show on the history of wine seen through 4,000 years in art. The wines are the expected Cabernet Sauvignon, Merlot and Chardonnay together with a traditional red Bordeaux blend.

Back on Highway 29 at the end of Dunaweal Lane, **Twomey Cellars** pours excellent Merlot and several different Pinot Noirs. This is a sister winery of Cabernet specialist Silver Oak. Twomey started life as a Merlot producer using the old French *soutirage* method of racking wine, employing gravity rather than pumps, perhaps the only winery in North America to do so. They have recently expanded into Pinot Noir production and produce some excellent single vineyard wines from Sonoma, Santa Barbara and Mendocino fruit.

One more winery of note in Calistoga is **Cuvaison** at the northern end of the Silverado Trail, just south of town. The tasting room is small and the wines are made from fruit grown in the Carneros and Mount Veeder AVAs, but they are well worth tasting. The Carneros Pinot Noir is especially good. Cuvaison has recently opened a modern tasting room and new winery in their Carneros Vineyards. Both tasting rooms serve the same vintages.

WINERIES & MORE

Chateau Montelena Winery
1429 Tubbs Lane
Calistoga, CA 94515
Tel: 707 942 5105
www.montelena.com
Open daily 9:30AM–4PM except major holidays. Check website for other closure dates.

Summers Estate Wines
1171 Tubbs Lane
Calistoga, CA 94515
Tel: 707-942-5508
www.summerswinery.com
Open Sun–Thurs 10:30AM–4:30PM,
Fri–Sat 10:30AM–5:30PM.

Schramsberg Vineyards
1400 Schramsberg Road
Calistoga, CA 94515
Tel: 707 942 4558
www.schramsberg.com
Open by appointment only. Check website for details.

Sterling Vineyards
1111 Dunaweal Lane
Calistoga, CA 94515-9635
Tel: 707 942 3344
www.sterlingvineyards.com
Open Mon–Fri 10:30AM–5PM,
Sat-Sun 10AM–5PM except major holidays.

Clos Pegase
1060 Dunaweal Lane
Calistoga, CA 94515
Tel: 707 942 4981.
www.clospegase.com
Open daily 10:30AM–5PM.

Twomey Cellars
1183 Dunaweal Lane
Calistoga, CA 94515
Tel: 800 505 4850
www.twomeycellars.com
Open Mon–Sat 9AM–5PM.
Closed Sundays.

Cuvaison Estate Wines
4550 Silverado Trail
Calistoga, CA 94515
Tel: 707 942 2468
www.cuvaison.com
Open daily 10AM–5PM.

ATTRACTIONS

Old Faithful Geyser of California
1299 Tubbs Lane
Calistoga, CA 94515-1055
Tel: 707 942 6463
www.oldfaithfulgeyser.com

Ca'Toga Galleria D'Arte
1206 Cedar Street
Calistoga, CA 94515
Tel: 707 942 3900
www.catoga.com
Open Thurs–Mon 11AM–6PM.

Villa Ca'Toga
3061 Myrtledale Road

Dutch Cape architecture distinguishes Chimney Rock Winery on Napa's Silverado Trail

Calistoga, CA 94515
Tel: 707 942 3900
Weekly tour Sat 11AM
May–Oct.

Wine Garage
1020 Foothill Blvd
Calistoga, CA 94515-1712
Tel: 707 942 5332
www.winegarage.net
Open Mon–Sat 11AM–
6:30PM, Sun 11AM–4:30PM.

The Silverado Trail

Locals know better than to fight summer traffic on Highway 29. They take the Silverado Trail that runs the length of Napa Valley from Napa Town for 30 miles north to Calistoga. Traffic can be so light that there is often the temptation to exceed the 55 mph limit, but be warned, there is always a heavy presence of the California Highway Patrol.

Although it's only a few miles east of Highway 29, the Silverado Trail is a world apart. In the 1800s it was a quiet horse path and the first winery was built in 1878. There are no towns along the route and only one store at the southern end of the trail at **Soda Canyon**. A handful of exclusive resorts are hidden from public view but wineries abound from ostentatious ego-massaging monuments to small boutique properties producing a few hundred cases a year. In those 30 miles you will find a sample of the whole gamut of Napa winery architecture.

At the southern end of the trail one of Napa's newest and most visually prominent wineries opened in 2004. **Darioush Winery** would look equally at home on the Las Vegas strip and the ornate architecture modeled after the ruins of Persepolis in Iran continues to receive criticism. How do

Stag's Leap Wine Cellars Cabernet Sauvignon established Napa Valley as a world-class producer when it won the legendary 1976 tasting in Paris.

the architects of these faux monuments feel copying ancient architects when they could be creating a California vernacular? Darioush is the dream of Darioush Khaledi, an Iranian businessman who made his fortune with a chain of discount stores in Southern California. On one hand this could not be further removed from Napa Valley but on the other, this genre of extravagant display is all too frequent. This extravagance goes beyond architecture. Darioush offers a tasting experience that has been described as the most astounding example of hospitality in Napa. For a significant fee ($300) you can participate in a two-hour wine experience that starts with caviar and Krug Champagne and ends with you selecting a bottle of wine from Khaledi's private cellar to be tasted alongside Darioush wines paired with **amuse-bouches** by Michelin-starred chef Ken Frank. **The Quintessential Wine Experience** is by appointment only.

Stags Leap district

Architectural aberrations aside, this is rural Napa at its best and the road passes some of the great vineyards of California. The Stags Leap district starts a short distance up the trail and is famous for Cabernet Sauvignon. Nathan Fey planted the first Cabernet vineyards as recently as 1961 and this fruit established the AVA as one of the premier regions. Fey planted 70 acres at a time when there were only 800 acres of Cabernet in the whole of the United States. Today there are more than 10,000 acres in Napa Valley alone.

Clos du Val is the first winery on the eastern side of the Trail as it passes through the Stags Leap district. Here they make elegant French-style wines that compete with the finest in the world. **Chimney Rock Winery** is the next stop and here the architecture is styled after the Cape of South Africa. The beautiful white façade stands out prominently from the surrounding vineyards. Although this is once again a copy of another style of architecture it does not seem out of place here, maybe because of its Southern Hemisphere wine country origins. Chimney Rock is a limited-production winery featuring high-end wines produced from estate fruit.

The winery that really put Stag's Leap on the map, and the whole California wine industry for that matter, is the appropriately named **Stag's Leap Wine-Cellars**, of Judgment of Paris fame, when their Cabernet Sauvignon beat the great French châteaux at the legendary 1976 blind tasting in Paris. The winery continues to produce outstanding Cabernets and is worth visiting for its importance in Napa wine history. The winery is a short distance past Chimney Rock and is easy to miss. The buildings are modest and hidden behind trees.

Almost directly across the road **Pine Ridge Winery** sources its fruit from five of Napa's top appellations to produce powerful California-style wines. The grounds provide a perfect picnic stop and tours of the winery include their 4,000-barrel cave.

Just north of Pine Ridge, you can find some of the best views of Napa Valley from the terrace of **Silverado Vineyards**, high on a knoll above their Cabernet Sauvignon vines. The winery is open during normal hours, and in the summer there are Friday evening terrace events, when seasonal small bites are served with award-winning wines. These events are by appointment only. Phone to check availability.

It's often difficult to differentiate between Napa winery experiences. Most produce and pour exceptionally good wines, many offer winery tours and an increasing number are offering food pairings. So what makes the difference? For a start, the varietal specialization of the winery, and then any attraction unique to the winery.

Stags Leap district ends at Yountville Cross Road and here are two wineries that merit a visit. **Robert Sinskey Winery** is one of the few biodynamically farmed wineries in the Valley and is totally committed to the "green" movement and sustainable farming. What also sets it apart is the emphasis on Pinot Noir from their vineyards in the Carneros District to the south. Most of the wineries of Stags Leap district specialize in Cabernet Sauvignon as their flagship offering but not Robert Sinskey. The food-pairing program here

Darioush Winery, modeled after the ancient city of Persepolis in Iran, typifies the often over-the-top architecture of many Napa wineries

is highly developed and provides one of the best experiences of its kind in Napa.

A short distance down Yountville Cross Road on the left, **Cliff Lede Winery** provides the only accommodation in the district. In addition there is a museum-quality art gallery and state-of-the-art tasting room.

Continue north on the Silverado Trail and just past Yountville Cross Road is a winery that rarely fails to impress visitors. **Paraduxx** is a member of the Duckhorn Wine Company and concentrates on red wines in the European tradition of blends created from authentic varietal pairings. The goal at Paraduxx has been to create distinctly Californian wines using Zinfandel blended with Cabernet Sauvignon and Merlot. The resulting wines have been outstanding and they are equaled by the overall tasting experience at the winery. Flights of wine are served with cheese either in the sleek, modern tasting room or under spreading walnut trees behind the winery. Reservations are necessary and these can be made online through Open Table.

The Silverado Trail continues past Oakville Cross Road into the heart of the Rutherford AVA. Vineyards extend across the Valley floor to the west and up steep hillsides to the east.

Most of the planting is Cabernet Sauvignon, which produces wine with a distinct earthy note from the "Rutherford dust" resulting from the volcanic deposits and a mixture of sand, gravel and loam. Some of the great Cabernet Sauvignons and Bordeaux blends come from here.

In a world of multinational corporate ownership of wineries, family-run wineries in Napa are becoming rarities but several of the best line the Silverado Trail. **ZD Wines** has been run by three generations of the de Leuze family and their Pinot Noir was the first wine to use the now acclaimed Carneros designation.

Almost next door to ZD, **Mumm Napa Valley** is the North American outpost of the great French Champagne house and they follow the company's tradition of making sparkling wines of finesse. The winery has a wonderful patio overlooking their vineyards and on warm summer days this is the perfect place to experience food and wine pairings. One of the great attractions of Mumm is their world-class photography gallery, which hosts several exhibitions throughout the year and is home to a collection of photographs by the great American landscape photographer Ansel Adams.

Sage Canyon Road

Sage Canyon Road winds up the eastern hills past Lake Hennessey and most of the wonderful cult, boutique wineries here are not open to the public. One winery, however, is open by appointment and is well worth the visit. Well-known restaurateur Pat Kuleto built his dream winery high above Napa Valley in 1993 but it looks as though it has been there forever. The gated entrance, about seven miles up Sage Canyon Road, is easy to miss. A small sign to **Kuleto Estate** confirms that this is the place and a code is needed to get through the massive wrought-iron gate almost hidden by trees on the left side of the road. A narrow road winds seemingly forever up the forested mountainside and you could be forgiven for thinking that you must have passed the winery somewhere along the way, but don't give up.

Paraduxx is known for its innovative blends of Napa varieties using Zinfandel as the base

At the top, the Tuscan architecture and expansive views over vineyards and Lake Hennessey make this one of the most memorable winery experiences in Napa. A major share in the winery was recently bought by Bill Foley to add to his already impressive portfolio.

Continue driving up Sage Canyon road for a couple of more miles to Number 3450 on the left. A sign announces **Somerston Vineyards**. This 1,680-acre property is planted with over 250 acres of vines in 87 blocks and is truly the last unexplored frontier of Napa Valley on the far eastern edge.

Remoteness and challenging terrain have helped keep this area undiscovered for so long. The vineyards lie between 900 and 2,400 feet above sea level, producing fruit that is both concentrated and elegant. These vineyards have been a source of contract fruit for many of Napa's great winemakers such as Heidi Barrett, and now Somerston is creating its own series of wines in a new production facility in the heart of the vineyards. The flocks of sheep grazing the hillsides above the vineyards provide a tempting source of food for the mountain lions that roam

Merlot grapes at Duckhorn Vineyards leave the destemmer on their way to the fermentation tanks

this wild location. Vineyard tours and al fresco tastings are available through their Yountville tasting room.

Back down on the Silverado Trail turn right and a short distance on the left a sleek, modern, crescent-shaped structure slices into the hillside above vineyards. **Quintessa** is the dream of Augustin Huneeus, a Chilean vintner who was previously president of Franciscan Estates. His dream was to create a winery that produced one singular estate wine from a single vineyard. The resulting wine justifies his effort.

Directly opposite, Rutherford Hill Road winds up to the exclusive **Auberg du Soleil** and its Michelin-starred restaurant, notable not only for exquisite food but also spectacular views over Napa Valley. Immediately past the resort is **Rutherford Hill Winery** sharing the same million-dollar valley view from their picnic area in an olive grove surrounded by oaks. The winery tour includes a walk through half a mile of underground caves and tastes of their signature Merlot and Cabernet Sauvignon.

The next stop should be **Duckhorn Vineyards**. Margaret and Dan Duckhorn built their winery's reputation on the currently unfashionable Merlot grape and their efforts have produced one of the best Merlots in North America. Duckhorn Cabernets also get high accolades.

Two very different family-owned and operated wineries sit across from each other on the Trail. Completely hidden from view at the end of a steep driveway, **Rombauer Vineyards** is a second-generation winery founded by ex-commercial airline pilot Koerner Rombauer. If the name rings a bell, Koerner's great-aunt was Irma Rombauer, who authored *The Joy of Cooking*. Koerner still runs the show; his son KR manages national sales and daughter Sheana manages public relations. Rombauer Chardonnay is their signature wine and deservedly popular.

Opposite Rombauer, **Failla** is a new and equally well-hidden winery named after owner and winemaker Ehren Jordan's wife. The Jordan name was taken by a very well-established winery in Sonoma's

Alexander Valley. Ehren Jordan is also winemaker for **Turley Wine Cellars** in Templeton on the Central Coast, where he crafts exceptional, and very expensive, Zinfandels. What sets Failla apart is the specialization on Pinot Noir—in a district known for Cabernet Sauvignon—and the charming, hunting lodge atmosphere of the tasting room. Visits are by appointment only and entering the tasting room is like visiting a private country cabin. The Pinot Noir, made from Sonoma Coast fruit, is exceptional, elegant and perfectly balanced.

The Silverado Trail continues north past vineyards and small wineries into Calistoga.

WINERIES & MORE

Clos du Val
5330 Silverado Trail
Napa, CA 94558-9410
Tel: 707 259 2200
www.closduval.com
Open daily 10AM–5PM.

Chimney Rock
5350 Silverado Trail
Napa, CA 94558
Tel: 707 257 2641
www.chimneyrock.com
Open daily 10AM–5PM.

Darioush
4240 Silverado Trail
Napa, CA 94558
Tel: 707 257 2345
www.darioush.com
Open daily 10:30AM–5PM.

Stag's Leap Cellars
6150 Silverado Trail
Napa, CA 94558
Tel: 800 640 5327
www.stagsleap.com
Open daily by
appointment.
(Book at least two
months ahead).

Pine Ridge Winery
5901 Silverado Trail
Napa, CA 94558-9417
Tel: 707 253 7500
www.pineridgewinery.com
Open daily 10:30–4:30
except major holidays.

Silverado Vineyards
6121 Silverado Trail
Napa, CA 94558
Tel: 707 257 1770
www.silveradovineyards.com
Open daily 10AM–5PM.

Robert Sinskey Winery
6320 Silverado Trail
Napa, CA 94558
Tel: 707 944 9090
www.robertsinskey.com
Open daily 10AM–4:30PM.

Somerston Vineyards
3450 Sage Canyon Road
St Helena, CA 94574
Tel: 707 967 8414
www.somerstonvineyards.com
By appointment only.

Cliff Lede Winery
1473 Yountville Cross Road
Yountville, CA 94599
Tel: 707 944 8642
www.cliffledevineyards.com
Open daily 10AM–4PM.

Paraduxx Winery
7257 Silverado Trail
Napa Valley, CA 94558
Tel: 866 367 9943
      707 945 0890
www.paraduxx.com
Open daily 10AM–4PM.

ZD Wines
8383 Silverado Trail
Napa, CA 94558
Tel: 707 963 5188
www.zdwines.com
Open daily 10AM–4:30PM.

Mumm Napa Valley
8445 Silverado Trail
Rutherford, CA 94573
Tel: 707 967 7700
www.mummnapa.com
Open daily 10AM–4:45PM
except major holidays.

Kuleto Estate Winery
2470 Sage Canyon Road
St Helena, CA 94574-9641
Tel: 707 302 2200

www.kuletoestate.com
Open daily by
appointment only.

Quintessa
PO Box 505
1601 Silverado Trail
Rutherford, CA 94573
Tel: 707 967 1601
www.quintessa.com
Open daily by appoint-
ment only 10AM–4PM.

Rutherford Hill Winery
200 Rutherford Hill Road
Rutherford, CA 94573
Tel: 707 963 1871
www.Rutherfordhill.com
Open daily 10AM–5PM
except major holidays.

Duckhorn Vineyards
1000 Lodi Lane
St Helena, CA 94574
Tel: 888 354 8885/
      707 963 7108
www.duckhorn.com
Open daily 10AM–4PM.

Rombauer Vineyards
3522 SilveradoTrail
St Helena, CA 94574
Tel: 707 963 5170
Open daily 10AM–5PM.

Failla
3530 Silverado Trail
St Helena, CA 94574
Tel: 707 963 0530
www.faillawines.com
By appointment only.

Los Carneros

Driving into Napa from Highway 101 you pass **Infineon Raceway**, and hopefully you will not be there on a day when the Nascar races are in full swing and the traffic outside the raceway comes to a stop.

Only a few years ago, for the next several miles the road passed sheep grazing land, hence the name Carneros (Spanish for "rams"). The land here has shallow soil that is not particularly fertile and grape growers didn't take long to realize that this is perfect terroir to grow high-quality fruit. Vines need to be stressed to produce grapes with great concentration and high acids that are ideal for winemaking. This terroir is further enhanced by the foggy mornings and cooling influence of the San Pablo Bay, creating ideal conditions for growing Pinot Noir and Chardonnay.

The Carneros AVA extends across two counties, Sonoma to the west and Napa to the east. This land, once believed to be fit only for grazing sheep, is now some of the most sought-after and expensive vineyard land in the state. Every plantable acre is covered in vines and within minutes of turning off Highway 37 you are obviously in wine country.

One of the first wineries north of San Francisco is in the Sonoma section of Los Carneros. Members of the Sebastiani family, who have been making wine in Sonoma for three generations, built Viansa to resemble a Tuscan hilltop villa. It is in fact far more than just a winery and the full name is **Viansa Winery and Italian Marketplace**.

Balloons fill the skies in the early morning in Napa Valley. A ride in a hot-air balloon is a great way to view Napa's vineyards

In spite of its prominent location and attractive setting the winery has been through difficult times but the quality of their wines has generally been maintained.

Across the road, **Cline Cellars** is notable for its red wines, particularly its old-vine Zinfandel. Several Rhône-style wines are made here, too, but most of the fruit comes from vineyards in Contra Costa County, an area not known for its viticulture. The tasting room is in an 1850s farmhouse surrounded by luxuriant gardens but its historic charm and understated atmosphere mask the fact that this is one of the first solar-powered wineries in California. Of particular interest is the display of a remarkable collection of scale models of all the missions of California. A team of German cabinetmakers originally made them for the World's Fair on Treasure Island in San Francisco Bay in 1939. Today, the models are acclaimed as an extraordinary and accurate depiction of California history. In 1998, the Cline family saved the models from being auctioned off individually and in 2005 created a museum behind the tasting room to showcase the collection.

The Jacuzzi family, of spa and hot tub fame, owns Cline Cellars and they have built a new winery directly across the road below Viansa. **Jacuzzi Family Vineyards** was modeled

Visitors taste the sparkling wines of the Napa outpost of the venerable Champagne GH Mumm & Cie

after the Jacuzzi family home in Udine, Italy, and in addition to the winery it is also home to **The Olive Press**, offering a different wine country experience through their tasting bar and a close-up view of their olive pressing facility. One of the more appealing aspects of Jacuzzi Family Vineyards is that tastings are offered free of charge.

About three miles north, a long driveway winds up through vineyards to **Gloria Ferrer Caves and Vineyard**. This sparkling wine house produces some of the best value sparkling wines in California, all made by the *méthode champenoise*. The Spanish cava producer Freixenet owns the winery, although that popular low-cost wine is not available here. Sparkling wine houses all seem to have wonderful tasting areas. Gloria Ferrer's terrace gives expansive views of Carneros out to the San Pablo Bay, a perfect place to spend a summer afternoon.

Highway 121 joins Highway 12 and vineyards cover the rolling hills for almost as far as the eye can see. Most of these are recent plantings and during spring brilliant yellow mustard flowers highlight the verdant landscape. Laura Chenel put America's goat cheese on the map at **Stornetta Dairy** in the historic buildings on Highway 12 just before the county line. Her legendary cheese is still made here although Laura sold the company in 2006.

The road sweeps down toward Napa Valley past vineyards that produce some of the world's greatest Chardonnay and Pinot Noir, such as **Hudson Vineyards** and **Winery Lake Vineyard**. Rene di Rosa sold Winery Lake several years ago and devoted his attention to his love of San Francisco Bay Area art. A flock of cutout sheep by the side of the road signals the entrance to the **di Rosa Preserve** (now known simply as di Rosa) that houses over 2000 works of art by 800 artists, spreading over 217 acres of land.

Directly across the highway from di Rosa is another California outpost of a European sparkling wine house. **Tattinger** is the parent company of Domaine Carneros and the faux château that was built in 1987 was, and still is in many circles, thought to be totally inappropriate for its imposing location on a knoll in the middle of Carneros. Whatever you may think of the building, the Champagne-style wines are excellent, with great finesse and delicacy. This is one of the most heavily trafficked tasting rooms in Napa not only because of the quality of the wines but for the terrace that looks out over di Rosa and surrounding vineyards.

Directly across from the entrance to Domaine Carneros, a long driveway leads to the Carneros tasting room of **Cuvaison Winery**. The original tasting room, which is still in operation, is on the Silverado Trail at Calistoga. The new facility, hidden from the road, is set overlooking rolling vineyards of Pinot Noir and Chardonnay and whether you sit inside or outside the views are equally impressive. The beautiful modern design of the building fits harmoniously into its setting and has "Napa Green" certification achieved through the extensive use of solar power.

Returning to Highway 12 and turning left onto Old Sonoma Highway and then left into Dealy Lane will eventually lead to

Artesa Winery and Vineyards, once again a winery located on high ground giving sweeping vineyard views from the inevitable tasting terrace. The winery itself is a wonderful example of contemporary architecture set behind fountains and sculptures. The property started out as a sparkling wine house under the name Codorniu Napa in 1991, but in 1997 the name was changed to Artesa and the focus shifted to still wines.

Return to Highway 12 and turn right onto Los Carneros Avenue. **Saintsbury** is an unimposing winery and it would be easy to dismiss it as unimportant by its physical presence. It is, however, the birthplace of some of the best Pinot Noir in the state. The founders, Dick Ward and David Graves, set out to make Burgundian-style Pinot from exclusively Carneros fruit, releasing their first wine in 1981, which put them in the forefront of the movement that would establish Carneros as a world-class winegrowing region.

Keep driving south toward San Pablo Bay and turn on Los Amigos Road.

Look for Buchi Station Road. Grapes were planted here in the mid-1800s, making this the site of the oldest continually operated winery in Los Carneros. **Bouchaine Vineyards** is the most recent of many incarnations of this winery property. Beringer Brothers owned the winery for 30 years before it was sold in 1981 to Gerret Copeland, who kept the old traditional open-top concrete fermentation tanks for Pinot Noir production. Michael Richmond, the founder of Acacia Winery, was hired as winemaker and general manager and his leadership has resulted in a new standard of excellence for their Pinot Noir and Chardonnay, which flourish in this cool climate region.

Pump over at Paraduxx Winery ensures optimal extraction by circulating the fermenting juice

Tel: 800 351 1133
www.vintageinn.com

RESTAURANTS

Ad Hoc
6476 Washington Street
Yountville, CA 94599
Tel: 707 944 2487
www.adhocrestaurant.com

Bistro Jeanty
6510 Washington Street
Yountville, CA 94599-1385
Tel: 707 944 0103
www.bistrojeanty.com

Bottega Ristorante
V Marketplace
6525 Washington Street
Yountville, CA 94599-1300
Tel: 707 945 1050
www.botteganapavalley.com

Bouchon
6534 Washington Street
Yountville, CA 94599
Tel: 707 944 8037
www.bouchonbistro.com

Brix
7377 St Helena Highway
Yountville, CA 94558
Tel: 707 944 2749
www.brix.com

French Laundry
6640 Washington Street
Yountville, CA 94599
Tel: 707 944 2380
www.frenchlaundry.com

Mustards Grill
(Between Yountville
and Oakville)
7399 St Helena Hwy
Napa, CA 94558-9726
Tel: 707 944-2424
www.mustardsgrill.com

Redd
6480 Washington Street
Yountville, CA 94599
Tel: 707 944 0447
www.reddnapavalley.com

St Helena

ACCOMODATIONS

El Bonita Motel
195 Main Street
St Helena, CA 94574
Tel: 800 541 3284
www.elbonita.com

Meadowood Napa Valley
900 Meadowood Lane
St Helena, CA 94574
Tel: 800 458 8080
www.meadowood.com

RESTAURANTS

Cindy's Backstreet Kitchen
1327 Railroad Avenue
Helena, CA 94574
Tel: 707 963 1200
cindysbackstreetkitchen.com

Go Fish
641 Main Street
St Helena, CA 94574
Tel: 707 963 0700
www.gofishreataurant.com

CARDINALE WINERY

Gott's Roadside
933 Main Street
St Helena, CA 94574
Tel: 707 963 3486
www.gottsroadside.com

Martini House
1245 Spring Street
St Helena, CA 94574
Tel: 707 963 2233
www.martinihouse.com

Terra
1345 Railroad Avenue
St Helena, CA 94574
Tel: 707 963 8931
www.terrarestaurant.com

Tra Vigne Restaurant
1050 Charter Oak Avenue
St Helena, CA 94574
Tel: 707 963 4444
www.travignerestaurant.com

Calistoga
ACCOMMODATIONS
Cottage Grove Inn
1711 Lincoln Avenue
Calistoga, CA 94515

Tel: 800 799 2284
www.cottagegrove.com

Mount View Hotel & Spa
1457 Lincoln Avenue
Calistoga, CA 94515
Tel: 800 816 6877
www.mountviewhotel.com

Solage Calistoga
755 Silverado Trail
Calistoga, CA 94515
Tel: 707 226 0850
www.solagecalistoga.com

RESTAURANT
JoLe
1457 Lincoln Avenue
Calistoga, CA 94515
Tel: 707 942 5938
www.jolerestaurant.com

Los Carneros
ACCOMMODATIONS
The Carneros Inn
4048 Sonoma Highway
Napa, CA 94559
Tel: 707 299 4900

WINE LABELS TO LOOK
FOR IN NAPA

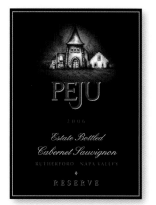

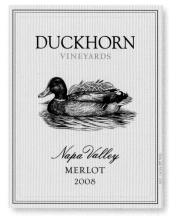

ESTD 1876

BERINGER.
PRIVATE RESERVE

CHARDONNAY

NAPA VALLEY

HESS.
COLLECTION

Mount Veeder | Napa Valley
CABERNET SAUVIGNON
2008

PINE RIDGE
VINEYARDS

2007

STAGS LEAP DISTRICT
CABERNET SAUVIGNON
NAPA VALLEY

ALC. 14.5% BY VOL.

ROBERT MONDAVI WINERY

2007

NAPA VALLEY
TO KALON VINEYARD
FUMÉ BLANC
RESERVE

THE
ORACLE

MINER
NAPA VALLEY RED WINE

HALL

Cabernet
Sauvignon
2006

Napa Valley

GRGICH HILLS
ESTATE

Napa Valley
CHARDONNAY
Estate 2008 Grown

STERLING
VINEYARDS.
RESERVE

CHARDONNAY
NAPA VALLEY

SONOMA COUNTY

MANY PEOPLE FEEL that Sonoma is like a breath of fresh air after the excesses of neighboring Napa. Unlike Napa, Sonoma is about far more than wine. Agriculture still plays a large role in the county with sheep farms, dairy herds, poultry farms and 76 miles of Pacific coastline with an active fishing industry. It is ranked as one of the most productive agricultural counties in the US.

Wine is big business, however. The county's 260 wineries produce 30 percent more wine than Napa from 60,000 acres under vine. The range of terroir is extremely varied, from the cool climates of Russian River and the Sonoma Coast, which produce exceptional Pinot Noirs and Chardonnays, to the heat of Dry Creek with great Zinfandels, Alexander Valley with a perfect climate for Cabernet Sauvignon and Sonoma Valley, home of the oldest operating commercial winery in America.

It's impossible to cover all of Sonoma County in one day. Although Sonoma Town is no further from San Francisco than Napa, the wineries are far more spread out and it's easy to spend a whole day in just one district.

Most of Sonoma's wineries are far less pretentious than those in Napa. There are a few grand estates, notably Kendall-Jackson, but most are simple working wineries, producing excellent wines at realistic prices. Most have tasting rooms and while there is still usually a charge it won't bankrupt you. Many of the wineries have picnic areas and on a summer day what could be more pleasant than sitting down with some local artisan cheeses, a loaf of sourdough bread and a wonderful bottle of wine straight from the cellar?

The county has 13 well-defined AVAs, each with its own distinct characteristics and dominant varietals. A few of

Tractor tours through the biodynamic vineyards at Benziger Vineyards are a popular attraction

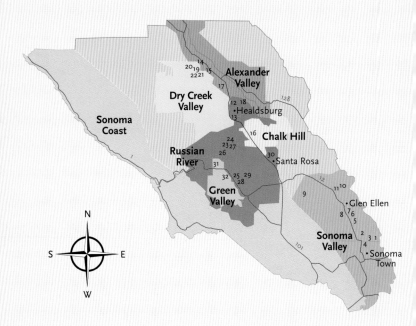

1. Buena Vista
2. Hanzell Vineyards
3. Ravenswood Winery
4. Sebastiani Vineyards & Winery
5. BR Cohn Winery
6. Arrowood Vineyards & Winery
7. Imagery Winery
8. Benziger Family Winery
9. Matanzas Creek Winery
10. Chateau St Jean Winery
11. Landmark Vineyards
12. Simi Winery
13. Seghesio Family Vineyards
14. Silver Oak Cellars
15. Geyser Peak Winery
16. Chalk Hill Estate
17. Francis Ford Coppola Winery
18. Jordan Vineyard & Winery
19. Ferrari-Carano Vineyards & Winery
20. Sbragia Family Vineyards
21. Preston Vineyards
22. Bella Vineyards
23. Williams Selyem Winery
24. Rochioli Vineyards & Winery
25. Dehlinger Winery
26. Gary Farrell Vineyards & Winery
27. Arista Winery
28. Lynmar Estate
29. DeLoach
30. Kendall Jackson Wine Center
31. Hartford Family Winery
32. Iron Horse Vineyards

WINE LABELS TO LOOK FOR IN SONOMA COUNTY

these regions consist primarily of vineyards supplying grapes to wineries in other areas and offer little of interest to the visitor other than beautiful scenery.

Santa Rosa

Highway 101 crosses the county and provides easy access to most of the main towns but the city of Santa Rosa has grown to a size where rush hour traffic can seriously clog the main roads.

Santa Rosa is the county seat and in the last few years the city has exploded to a population of over 170,000 with over 500,000 people living in the greater metropolitan area. There is little reason to stop in Santa Rosa. The small-town, agricultural settlement has grown into a sprawling city that regrettably has little character. The main reason to stop here is for reasonably priced accommodation that is ideally located for exploration of the surrounding wine country.

The only historic neighborhood is **Railroad Square**, an area of pre-1906 earthquake buildings that now houses a few blocks of restaurants and antique shops. There are two attractions worthy of attention.

Santa Rosa was home to horticulturalist **Luther Burbank**, who pioneered hybridization and developed hundreds of new varieties of fruits and flowers including the plumcot and Shasta daisy. His house and gardens are open to the public and are designated as a National Historic Landmark.

More recently the city was also home for over 40 years to Charles M Schulz, who created Peanuts. In 2002, two years after his death, the **Charles M Schultz Museum** opened as a memorial to one of the world's greatest cartoonists. The museum houses a permanent exhibit of original drawings and memorabilia together with thematic exhibits that examine how Schultz developed his characters. A museum of comic strips may not sound too exciting but this one is definitely worth a side trip.

Sonoma Town

Sonoma is the birthplace of California's wine industry. This charming old town, arranged around a tradi-

The plaza in **Sonoma Town** is a perfect place to stroll, shop and stop for refreshments

tional plaza, is steeped in history. Here is the last of California's missions, built in 1823 and connected by the Camino Real that parallels Highway 101. It's no coincidence that this route still connects all the wine regions because it was the Jesuits who brought **vinifera** to California to make wine.

For a short time in 1846 Sonoma was the capital of the California Republic and the birthplace of American California. Most of the buildings associated with this era still stand around the plaza. The eight-acre plaza is the largest in California and has been designated a National Historic Landmark.

Most of the buildings surrounding the plaza are open to the public: Mission San Francisco Solano; Presidio of Sonoma; the Swiss Hotel that was the original home of General Vallejo's brother; and the Blue Wing Inn that is now a museum. A short distance from the plaza is Lachryma Montis, General Vallejo's home, which is also a museum. All these historic sites fall under the umbrella of **Sonoma State Historic Park** and one ticket gives entrance to all the properties.

This concentration of history has made Sonoma a popular tourist destination but the traffic never seems to reach the levels of Highway 29 in neighboring Napa Valley. Shops and restaurants rub shoulders with the historic buildings around the Plaza and several wineries are just a few minutes away.

Buena Vista is particularly notable for being the first commercial winery in the state, founded in 1857 by Agoston Haraszthy, the father of California viticulture. (He is also credited with the introduction of the Zinfandel grape, although this attribution is questionable. Gold miners in Amador County most likely introduced it some years earlier.) The winery is still housed in the original stone buildings.

Sebastiani Vineyards and Winery, only a couple of blocks from the Plaza, was established by Italian immigrant Samuele Sebastiani in 1904. This was the only winery in Sonoma County to continue production through Prohibition by making sacramental and medicinal wines. The winery was in family ownership until 2008 when vintner Bill Foley added the property to his already impressive portfolio. A collection of hand-carved oak barrels is a highlight of the winery tour.

Back up on the hill above Sonoma past Sebastiani, Joel Peterson started **Ravenswood Winery** in 1976. He started with Zinfandel and has continued to make some of the best single-vineyard Zinfandels around. Other varietals have been added to the inventory but it's still

« Sonoma Valley extends south from Santa Rosa to Sonoma Town and was home to both the novelist Jack London and writer MFK Fisher

the Zins that shine. The winery motto "No Wimpy Wines" sums up the Raven-swood approach to win-emaking. The winery was sold to the giant Constel-lation Brands but Peterson remains at the helm.

Another historically significant winery is hid-den away at the western end of town. Ambassador James Zellerbach pur-chased 200 acres of land just one mile from So-noma Plaza to create a small vineyard and winery dedicated to producing Burgundian-style Pinot Noir and Chardonnay. He planted the first six acres of Pinot in 1953 in what is now the oldest Pinot Noir vineyard in America. The gravity-fed winery is a $2/3$-scale replica of Clos de Vougeot in Burgundy and although the architec-ture and ideals followed traditional Burgundian values the winemaking was state of the art and many innovative techniques were introduced which have become the standard for modern winemaking. Stainless-steel tanks were first introduced here, as was induced malolactic fermen-tation for Chardonnay. Since those early days the property has been through three different ownerships and the original vineyard has grown to 42 acres. This is not terroir where you expect to find great Pinot Noir but **Hanzell Vine-yards** continues to produce outstanding wines.

Sonoma Valley

This valley is the historic home of the California wine industry, and is protected from the wet and cool ef-fects of the Pacific Ocean by Sonoma Mountain. The wineries now lining the val-ley produce a wide variety of wines of very high quality.

North out of town on Highway 12, passing through **Boyes Hot Springs** on your way to the valley proper, the charm of down-town Sonoma evaporates into characterless suburbs. **BR Cohn Winery** soon appears on the west side of the road. Bruce Cohn was manager of the Doobie Brothers before he opened his eponymous winery in 1984. He has expanded his business to include the production of gourmet olive oil and vinegars.

A couple of miles further up Highway 12, a driveway off to the east leads to two

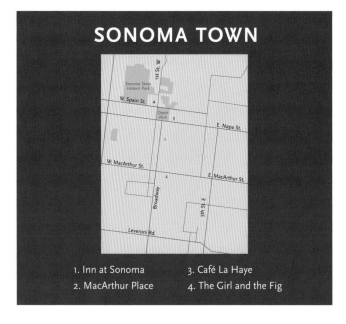

SONOMA TOWN

1. Inn at Sonoma
2. MacArthur Place
3. Café La Haye
4. The Girl and the Fig

very different wineries. **Arrowood Winery** is housed in a southern-style wooden house with verandas overlooking estate vineyards. Richard Arrowood released his first wine in 1988. The winery sources fruit from the best vineyards in Sonoma County and although the winery was bought by Robert Mondavi, which then morphed into the giant Constellation Brands, the quality of the wine has been maintained.

The driveway to Arrowood splits off to the left and leads to a modern post-industrial-style building that couldn't be more different from its neighbor. The winery dates back to the early 1980s as the baby of Joe Benziger of the Benziger family, who at that time was making big-production wines under the Glen Ellen label. Joe decided that some of their fruit deserved better treatment and **Imagery** was born. From the start, Joe used original art for the Imagery labels and one of the attractions at the winery is a collection of works from many internationally respected artists who have designed Imagery labels.

Glen Ellen

Continuing north on Highway 12 turn left on to Arnold Drive, which leads to Glen Ellen. The town has only 1,000 residents and its greatest claim to fame is as the home of writer Jack London. What is now **Jack London State Park** was London's home until his death in 1916 and the original buildings are open to the public, including the **House of Happy Walls** and the ruins of the **Wolf House**. Vineyards surround the park and a very pleasant afternoon can be spent horseback riding through the vineyards.

Benziger Family Winery is hidden from view as you drive up London Ranch Road to the State park. A long driveway leads past vineyards to the winery. The Benzigers are enthusi-

astic supporters of organic and biodynamic farming. They are convinced this is the road to better wine and that if the land is in balance, so will be the wines. A tram ride gives a close-up look at their biodynamic vineyards and the tour clearly illustrates the benefits of responsible vineyard management.

Warm Springs Road leaves Glen Ellen and turns into Bennett Valley Road. During early summer this detour to **Matanzas Creek Winery** is worthwhile if only to view the spectacular lavender gardens that cascade down from the secreted winery building. The wines are pretty good,

Chalk Hill AVA gets its name from the chalky white volcanic soil that lends itself to growing white wine varieties

too, and cover the usual suspects: Cabernet Sauvignon, Merlot, Syrah, Pinot Noir, Chardonnay and Sauvignon Blanc. So what else is new! Fruit is sourced throughout Sonoma County and the winery is now part of Jackson Family Wines. Yes, that Jackson. Jess.

Return to Highway 12 and turn left to travel north. In Kenwood, **Chateau St Jean** is the most splendid winery in southern Sonoma. Set in beautifully landscaped grounds, the original chateau was built in 1920 as the summer home of the Goff family from Michigan and is now listed in the National Trust for Historic Preservation. The wines are as grand as the buildings with several single vineyard wines and reserve blends that cover the gamut of grape varieties.

Just past Chateau St Jean, Adobe Canyon Road intersects Highway 12. Turn right and stop at **Landmark Vineyards**, which was one of the first wineries in the state to concentrate primarily on Chardonnay. The Spanish mission-style winery was built by the great-great-granddaughter of John Deere, the inventor of the steel plow and founder of the company that

now dominates worldwide agricultural equipment manufacture. Beautiful landscaped gardens allow picnics and a bocce ball court is available for visitors. A horse-drawn wagon gives tours of the grounds on summer weekends.

Chalk Hill

Just north of Santa Rosa, Chalk Hill AVA sits along the western slopes of the Mayacamus Mountains, close to the commuter settlement of Windsor. It is in the northeast corner of the Russian River AVA but the climate here is much warmer due to a thermal belt that runs through the region. The white color of the soil comes from the quartzite-laden volcanic ash from eruptions of Mount St Helena, creating perfect conditions for stressing vines to produce concentrated fruit. There is no chalk in sight. The only winery of significance in the AVA is appropriately **Chalk Hill Winery** and it is one of the most impressive wine estates in California, covering 1,477 acres with 350 acres of vineyards. Fred Furth, who made a fortune as a trial lawyer, founded the winery in 1980 and the estate is magnificent. It has its own chapel, an equestrian arena and beautifully manicured hillsides of vines. The wines include Cabernet Sauvignon, Merlot, Syrah, Chardonnay, Sauvignon Blanc and Pinot Gris. They are all first-class wines. Furth sold the estate to Bill Foley in 2010.

Healdsburg

The town of Healdsburg is the jewel of Sonoma wine country. Once a sleepy country town arranged around a quaint tree-lined plaza, it's been transformed into a hip destination with Michelin-starred restaurants, trendy boutiques and expensive boutique hotels. Bed and breakfast inns are a popular, if pricey, alternative. The gentrification of Healdsburg has certainly pushed up prices but fortunately the underlying character of the town hasn't been disturbed. Any small town that can support two independent bookstores can't be bad. Grab a fresh fruit tart from **Downtown Bakery**, sit under the trees in the plaza on a warm summer day and you may never want to leave.

One of the year's main events is the annual **Jazz Festival** held in June. Throughout the summer a farmers' market is held on Tuesday evening and Saturday morning. All the producers must be within a ten-mile radius of Healdsburg.

Simi Winery on Healdsburg Avenue was founded in 1876 and remained in Simi family ownership until 1970. In 1979 acclaimed winemaker Zelma Long modernized the winery, and in 1985 Simi became the first US winery to hire another wine legend, French winery consultant Michel Roland.

A quiet Healdsburg backstreet is home to **Seghesio Family Vineyards**. Since 1902, the Seghesios have been making some of the best Zinfandels in California, mostly from estate fruit.

Alexander Valley

Highway 101 is the main artery through the Alexander Valley, which extends from Cloverdale on the Mendocino County line down to Healdsburg. Vineyards extend as far as the eye can see on either side of the freeway and are the source of some

Alexander Valley's Jimtown Store elevates the classic country store to gourmet destination filled with antiques

of the best Cabernet Sauvignon grapes in the State.

Silver Oak Cellars' Alexander Valley winery is the fraternal twin of the Napa Valley property. When Justin Meyer and Ray Duncan founded Silver Oak in Napa in 1972 they sourced their fruit from Alexander Valley. However, it wasn't until 1992 that they established a physical presence in Sonoma when they bought the old Lyeth Winery property. Silver Oak only makes Cabernet Sauvignon in a style that is in perfect balance on release. It is always aged in American oak, giving the wine a distinctive character. The winery is highly visible on the west side of Highway 101 but is not so easy to get to. Take the Canyon Road exit off 101, turn right on Chianti Road on the west side of the freeway and continue for three miles to the winery.

On the way to Silver Oak, just as you turn onto Chianti Road, one of the oldest wineries in the county is on the left. **Geyser Peak Winery** was founded in 1880 and produces Cabernet Sauvignon, Sauvignon Blanc and Chardonnay, together with a few other varietals and blends. Australian winemaker Daryl Groom crafted the wines in the 1990s and established Geyser Peak as an important player in the market. Groom has long gone but in spite of ownership changes the quality of the wines has not diminished.

Continuing south on Highway 101, you will come to **Chateau Souvrain**, housed in a distinctive hop kiln-inspired building just off the freeway, which was bought by filmmaker Francis Ford Coppola. He modestly renamed it **Francis Ford Coppola Winery**! It opened in late 2010 and the goal is to make it a destination winery with a full-service restaurant and family activities. The jury is still out on the quality of the wines.

Jordan Winery, at the southern end of Alexander Valley, is perhaps the closest you can get to the experience of visiting a great French wine estate. The ivy-covered buildings and manicured gardens echo the quality and care that winemaker Rob Davies puts into the exceptional Cabernet Sauvignon and Chardonnay estate wines.

A short distance down Alexander Valley Road, **Jimtown Store** presents a world of whimsical souvenirs, antiques and a gourmet deli in an authentic old-time country store setting.

Dry Creek Valley

West of Alexander Valley is Dry Creek Valley, and here Zinfandel is king. This uniquely Californian grape thrives in the warm temperatures of Dry Creek, producing big, fruity wines. Many of the wineries are small, family operations but **Ferrari Carano** is as splendid as anything in Napa and the gardens alone are worth the visit. Reno, Nevada lawyer and casino owner Don Carano, with his wife Rhonda, built the winery in 1985. The wines are made from fruit from several northern California appelations with an emphasis on Italian style.

A couple of miles up Dry Creek Road, Ed Sbragia, the former winemaker for Beringer Vineyards in Napa Valley, recently opened **Sbragia Family Vineyards** in a property at the head of the valley with spectacular views over vineyards and Lake Sonoma. The wines are as good as you would expect from the man who

<< The barrel room at Ridge Vineyards Lytton Springs winery. Lytton Springs became part of the Ridge estate in 1991

The Russian River carves through its eponymous AVA, one of Sonoma County's premier Pinot Noir regions

established Beringer as a world-class winery.

On the west side of Dry Creek are two small wineries that are very different in character but equally worth a visit. **Preston Vineyards'** founder, Lou Preston, is one of the great vintners of Sonoma, and totally committed to organic agriculture. As you may expect from a self-proclaimed aging hippie, his approach is holistic. Organic produce and a bakery compliment the wines. Their tasting room experience is regularly rated as one of the best in America.

A little farther on from Preston, at the end of the road, **Bella Vineyards** is worth a visit if only for the experience of their unique tasting room deep in their wine cave.

Russian River

Russian River is a much cooler region than neighboring Dry Creek because of the marine influence, which creates foggy, cool mornings and evenings. This is the source of great Pinot Noir fruit and some of the greatest names call this home. Williams Selyem, Rochioli, Delinger, Gary Farrell and many more are making exceptional wines. Chardonnay also grows well here.

Some of the most notable Pinot Noir wineries are not open to the public but there are still enough great ones to fill a couple of days.

Rochioli is one of the flagship Pinot wineries and their modest tasting room is a mecca for Pinot lovers. Don't be surprised if they are not pouring your favorite Pinot, however. Most of their Pinots sell out on release and you may have to settle for Chardonnay or Sauvignon Blanc.

Across from Rochioli, a short distance down Westside Road, **Arista Winery** is the new kid on the block. The McWilliams family from Texas started the winery in 2004 and they are already making elegant Pinot Noirs that belie their youthful origins.

Gary Farrell is synonymous with Russian River Pinot Noir. The winery bearing his name however has been sold twice since he established it in 2000. It was set up to make single-vineyard Pinot Noir but the current owners have expanded into other varietals including Zinfandel and Merlot.

Lynmar Estate offers elegant wine and food pairings in their modern tasting room or, even better, on the terrace overlooking the estate vineyards. They specialize in estate-grown Pinot Noir and Chardonnay.

DeLoach was a Russian River winery that made good, solid wines that were rarely distinguished. Their Zinfandel was particularly notable. Then along came Jean-Charles Boisset of the great Burgundian wine family who bought the property and made it into a showcase for Pinot Noir. There is an emphasis on sustainable farming and organic practices.

Martinelli is a well-known American brand of non-alcoholic apple cider but don't be confused. **Martinelli Winery** has no connection with this fizzy drink. The Martinelli family has been growing grapes in the Russian River Valley since 1887 and they produce very high quality Pinot Noir, Chardonnay, Zinfandel and Syrah from their estate vineyards. Their wines are unfined, unfiltered and are neither cold nor heat stabilized. Legendary Helen Turley is their consultant winemaker.

No round-up of Russian River would be complete without mentioning **Kendall Jackson**. Jess Jackson cemented his success with an oaked Chardonnay that took the American palate by storm. This simple, accessible white wine became one of the biggest sellers in the country. In more recent years, Jackson has been acquiring quality properties such as Cardinale, La Jota and Freemark Abbey in Napa; Matanzas Creek, Hartford Court and

Stonestreet in Sonoma and Cambria in Santa Barbara County. The flagship however is the Kendall Jackson Wine Center just north of Santa Rosa next to Highway 101. This faux chateau not only is a showcase for the KJ wines but the culinary and sensory gardens spreading over 120 acres provide an added dimension to the wine country adventure. Food pairings are an important element of the KJ tasting experience and every autumn the winery hosts a weekend-long heirloom tomato festival that has become a highlight of California's culinary calendar.

Green Valley

This is really a sub-appellation of Russian River Valley just to the north of Sebastopol. It is even cooler than

Traditional *soutirage* is used to decant Merlot from barrel to barrel at Twomey in Napa. This process oxygenates the wine

It's difficult to get lost on the backroads of Sonoma County, as the majority of wineries are well, if discreetly, signposted

the surrounding Russian River AVA and is a source of premium Pinot fruit.

Hartford Court, a winery founded by Jess Jackson's son-in-law, Don Hartford, produces several outstanding, single-vineyard Pinot Noirs. Although the winery only dates back to 1993, the classical building, set among trees in the heart of Green Valley, could have been there for centuries.

The Sterling family established **Iron Horse** Vineyards in 1976 on a site that many considered too problematic to grow grapes, with frost occurring as late as June.

At the time this was the most westerly vineyard in California. However, the Sterlings recognized this as ideal Chardonnay and Pinot Noir terroir and for over 30 years produced outstanding sparkling wines that have been served at the White House for five consecutive presidential administrations.

Sonoma Coast

This huge appellation of over half a million acres begs definition. It extends from the Mendocino County line all the way down to Marin County to the south. The unifying characteristic is its proximity to the coast as its name suggests and although the area is generally cool, with such a vast area terroir varies dramatically. In the north, spectacular vineyards spread over mountain tops at well over 1,000 feet above the Pacific Ocean, while in the south the vineyards carpet the relatively low, flat areas adjacent to Los Carneros. Again, Burgundian varietals, Pinot Noir and Chardonnay, predominate.

Some of the best Pinot Noir fruit comes from the northern vineyards and

these growers and wineries have coined the name TRUE Sonoma Coast to differentiate them from the vineyards to the south. Many of these TRUE Sonoma Coast vineyards are well hidden and closed to the public. **Flowers, Hirsch, Marcassan** and **Peay** all have spectacular vineyards producing outstanding fruit but it could take you weeks to find them even if you could eventually pass through the locked gates.

WINERIES & MORE

Buena Vista
18000 Old Winery Road
Sonoma, CA 95476
Tel: 707 265 1472
www.buenavistacarneros.com
Open daily 10AM–5PM.

Hanzell Vineyards
18596 Lomita Ave
Sonoma, CA 95476
Tel: 707 996 3860
www.hanzell.com
By appointment only.

Ravenswood Winery
18701 Gehricke Road
Sonoma, CA 95476
Tel: 888 669 4679
www.ravenswoodwinery.com
Open daily 10AM–4:30PM.

Sebastiani Vineyards
& Winery
389 Fourth Street East
Sonoma, CA 95476
Tel: 707 933 3230
www.sebastiani.com
Open daily 10AM–5PM.

Arrowood Vineyards
& Winery
14347 Highway 12
Glen Ellen, CA 95442
Tel: 707 935 2600
www.arrowoodvineyards.com
Open daily 10AM–4:30PM.

BR Cohn Winery
15000 Sonoma Highway
Glen Ellen, CA 95442
Tel: 800 330 4064
www.brcohn.com
Open daily 10AM–5PM.

Imagery Winery
14335 Highway 12
Glen Ellen, CA 95442
Tel: 707 935 4515
www.imagerywinery.com
Open Mon-Fri

This ornately-carved fermentation tank is one of the highlights of a visit to Sebastiani Vineyards in Sonoma

10AM–4:30PM,
Sat-Sun 10AM–5:30PM.

Benziger Family Winery
1883 London Ranch Road
Glen Ellen, CA 95442
Tel: 707 935 3000
www.benziger.com
Open daily 10AM–5PM.

Matanzas Creek Winery
6097 Bennett Valley Road
Santa Rosa, CA 95404
Tel: 707 528 6464
www.matanzascreek.com
Open daily 10:30AM–4:30PM.

Chateau St Jean Winery
8555 Sonoma Highway
Kenwood, CA 95452-9026
Tel: 707 833 4134
www.chateaustjean.com
Open daily 10AM–5PM
except major holidays.

Landmark Vineyards
101 Adobe Canyon Road
Kenwood, CA 95452
Tel: 707 833 0053
www.landmarkwine.com
Open daily 10:30AM–4:30PM.

Simi Winery
16275 Healdsburg Avenue
Healdsburg, CA 95448
Tel: 707 433 3686
www.simiwinery.com
Open daily 10AM–5PM.

Seghesio Family Vineyards
14730 Grove Street
Healdsburg, CA 95448
Tel: 707 433 3579
www.seghesio.com
Open daily 10AM–5PM
except major holidays.

Silver Oak Cellars
24625 Chianti Road
Geyserville, CA 95441
Tel: 707 942 7026
www.silveroak.com
Open Mon-Sat 9AM–5PM.
Closed Sun and some
holidays.

Geyser Peak Winery
22281 Chianti Road
Geyserville, CA 95441
Tel: 707 857 2500
www.geyserpeakwinery.com
Open daily 10AM–5PM
except major holidays.

Chalk Hill Estate
10300 Chalk Hill Road
Healdsburg, CA 95448
Tel: 707 838 4837
www.chalkhill.com
Tours by appointment
only.

Francis Ford Coppola Winery
300 Via Archimedes
Geyserville, CA 95441
Tel: 707 857 1400
www.franciscoppolawinery.com
Open daily 11AM–5PM.

Jordan Vineyard & Winery
1474 Alexander
Valley Road
Healdsburg, CA 95448
Tel: 707 431 5250
www.jordanwinery.com
Open Mon-Fri 8AM–
4:30PM, Sat-Sun 9AM–
3:30PM. Closed Sun
Nov-Apr and major
holidays.

Ferrari-Carano Vineyards & Winery
8761 Dry Creek Road
Healdsburg, CA 95448
Tel: 707 433 6700
www.ferrari-carano.com
Open daily 10AM–5PM.

Sbragia Family Vineyards
9990 Dry Creek Road
Geyserville, CA 95441
Tel: 707 473 2992
www.sbragia.com
Open daily 11AM–5PM.

Preston Vineyards
9282 West Dry Creek Road
Healdsburg, CA 95448
Tel: 707 433 3372
www.prestonvineyards.com
Open daily 11AM–4:30PM.

Bella Vineyards
9711 West Dry Creek Road
Healdsburg, CA 95448
Tel: 866 572 3552
www.bellawinery.com
Open daily 11AM–4:30PM.

SILVER OAK WINERY

Williams Selyem Winery
6575 Westside Road
Healdsburg, CA 95448
Tel: 707 433 6425
www.williamsselyem.com
Tours by appointment.
Minimum two weeks'
notice.

Rochioli Vineyards & Winery
6192 Westside Road
Healdsburg, CA 95448
Tel: 707 433 2305
www.rochioliwinery.com
Open Thurs-Mon
11AM–4PM Tues, Wed
by appointment only.

Dehlinger Winery
4101 Vine Hill Road
Sebastopol, CA 95472
Tel: 707 823 2378
www.dehlingerwinery.com
Open by appointment
Fri only.

**Gary Farrell
Vineyards & Winery**
10701 Westside Road
Healdsburg, CA 95448
Tel: 707 473 2900
www.garyfarrellwines.com
Open daily 10:30AM–4.30PM
except major holidays.

Arista Winery
7015 Westside Road
Healdsburg, CA 95448
Tel: 707 473 0606
www.aristawinery.com
Open daily 11AM–5PM.

Lynmar Estate
3909 Frei Road
Sebastopol, CA 95472
Tel: 707 829 3374
www.lynmarwinery.com
Open daily 10AM–5PM.

DeLoach
1791 Olivet Road
Santa Rosa, CA 95401
Tel: 707 526 9111
www.deloachvineyards.com
Open daily 10AM–5PM
except major holidays.

**Kendall Jackson
Wine Center**
5007 Fulton Road
Santa Rosa, CA 95403
Tel: 707 571 8100
www.kj.com
Open daily 10AM–5PM.

Hartford Family Winery
8075 Martinelli Road
Forestville, CA 95436
Tel: 707 887 8010
www.hartfordwines.com
Open daily 10AM–4:30PM.

Iron Horse Vineyards
9786 Ross Station Road
Sebastopol, CA 95472
Tel: 707 887 1507
www.ironhorsevineyards.com
Open daily 10AM–3:30PM.

ATTRACTIONS
**Luther Burbank's
House**
Santa Rosa Ave
and Sonoma Ave
Santa Rosa, CA 95401
Tel: 707 524 5445
www.lutherburbank.org
Open daily 8AM–dusk.

**Charles M Schulz
Museum**
2301 Hardies Lane
Santa Rosa, CA 95403
Tel: 707 579 4452
www.schulzmuseum.org
See website for opening
hours.

Jimtown Store
6706 Highway 128
Healdsburg, CA 95448
Tel: 707 433 1212
www.jimtown.com
See website for opening
hours.

WHERE TO STAY AND EAT

Santa Rosa

ACCOMODATIONS

Flamingo Conference
Resort and Spa
2777 Fourth Street
Santa Rosa, CA 95409
Tel: 707 545 8530
www.flamingoresort.com

Fountaingrove Inn
101 Fountaingrove Parkway
Santa Rosa, CA 95403
Tel: 707 578 6101
www.fountaingroveinn.com

RESTAURANTS

John Ash & Co Restaurant
4330 Barnes Road
Vintners Inn
Santa Rosa, CA 95403
Tel: 707 527 7687
www.vintnersinn.com/
johnash.asp

Syrah Bistro
205 5th Street
Santa Rosa, CA 95401
Tel: 707 568 4002
www.syrahbistro.com

Sonoma

ACCOMODATIONS

Inn at Sonoma
630 Broadway
Sonoma, CA 95476
Tel: 888 568 9818
www.innatsonoma.com

MacArthur Place
29 East MacArthur Street
Sonoma, CA 95476
Tel: 800 722 1866
www.macarthurplace.com

RESTAURANTS

Café La Haye
140 East Napa Street
Sonoma, CA 95476
Tel: 707 935 5994
www.cafelahaye.com

The Girl and the Fig
110 West Spain Street
Sonoma, CA 95476
Tel: 707 938 3634
www.thegirlandthefig.com
Californian/French cuisine

Healdsburg

ACCOMODATIONS

Duchamp Hotel
421 Foss Street
Healdsburg, CA 95448
Tel: 707 431 1300
www.duchamphotel.com

H2 Hotel
219 Healdsburg Avenue
Healdburg, CA 95448
Tel: 707 922 5251
www.h2hotel.com

Hotel Healdsburg
25 Matheson Street
Healdsburg, CA 95448
Tel: 800 889 7188
www.hotelhealdsburg.com

HEALDSBURG
DELI

RESTAURANTS

Cyrus Restaurant
29 North Street
Healdsburg, CA 95448
Tel: 707 433 3311
wnww.cyrusrestaurant.com
Californian/French cuisine

Madrona Manor
1001 Westside Road
Healdsburg, CA 95448
Tel: 707 433 4231
www.madronamanor.com

**Zin Restaurant
and Wine Bar**
344 Center Street
Healdsburg, CA 95448
Tel: 707 473 0946
www.zinrestaurant.com

Guerneville

ACCOMODATIONS

Applewood Inn
13555 Highway 116
Guerneville, CA 95446
Tel: 707 869 9093
www.applewoodinn.com

Sebastopol

RESTAURANT

K & L Bistro
119 South Main Street
Sebastopol, CA 95472
Tel: 707 823 6614
www.klbistro.com
French cuisine

MENDOCINO COUNTY

MENDOCINO is rapidly becoming an important player in the California wine world. Whether it's because of global warming or astronomical land prices in Napa and Sonoma, the fact remains that world-class wines are now being produced here.

The county has always been a sparsely populated rural area with an economy revolving around a highly profitable but also highly illegal cash crop. It will be interesting to see what happens if marijuana is ever legalized. Leaving Sonoma County's Alexander Valley, Highway 101 bisects Mendocino on its way up to Humboldt County and eventually to Oregon. Several wineries line this corridor but the jewel of the county is Anderson Valley, which has become renowned for the quality of its Pinot Noir. The valley has a feeling of remoteness generated by difficulty of access. All roads into Anderson Valley are winding and steep and although it's only an hour's drive from Highway 101 it feels like entering another world. The only town, Boonville, was so isolated that it developed its own dialect called Boontling, which lingers to this day.

Mendocino Town

The rugged Pacific coast is the highlight of Mendocino County and by far the biggest attraction is its eponymous town, jutting out into the Pacific. Mendocino is a charming Victorian arts community notable for its starring role in the television series *Murder She Wrote*, in which it represents a coastal New England village. If you like art galleries and trendy boutiques this is the place for you but don't expect big-city sophistication. The town has

« **An old water tower at Handley Cellars, a small family-owned winery near Philo in Anderson Valley**

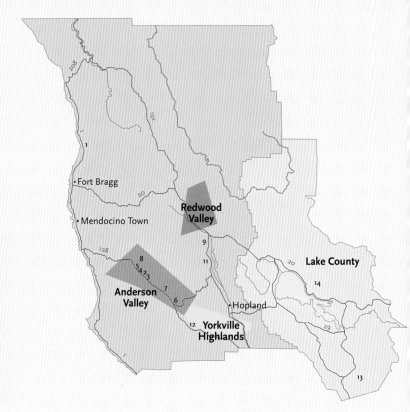

Redwood Valley

Lake County

Anderson Valley

Yorkville Highlands

Fort Bragg

Mendocino Town

Hopland

1. Pacific Star Winery
2. Husch Vineyards
3. Navarro Vineyards
4. Roederer Estate
5. Handley Cellars
6. Londer Vineyards Tasting Room
7. Breggo Cellars
8. Esterlina Vineyards & Winery
9. Parducci Wine Cellars
10. Jeriko Estate Winery
11. Germain-Robin
12. Maple Creek Winery
13. Langtry Estate and Vineyards
14. Brassfield Estate Winery

WINE LABELS TO LOOK FOR IN MENDOCINO COUNTY

fewer than 1,000 permanent residents but its population can more than double in size during the tourist season and, as with any town full of Victorian houses, bed and breakfast inns abound.

Fort Bragg

A few miles to the north, Fort Bragg, with a population of about 8,000, is the second biggest town in the county. It started life as a military outpost in 1856, eventually morphed into a lumber town and the utilitarian atmosphere still persists. What Fort Bragg lacks in charm is made up for by **Noyo Harbor** at the southern end of town. This active fishing port is the center for the Dungeness crab industry and also salmon fishing, when in season. Sports fishing is the main tourist attraction but be warned, the waters outside the harbor can get pretty choppy.

The western terminus of the California Western Railroad is still in operation but instead of logs the train now transports tourists through redwood forests between Fort Bragg and Willets on what is now known as the **Skunk Train**. Continuing north for 12 miles you come to the most westerly winery in California. **Pacific Star Winery** sits right by the ocean and owner and winemaker Sally Otterson claims that the salt from sea air deposits on barrels accelerates osmosis and creates viscous and dense wines. The winery may appear to be an oddity but the wines deserve serious attention.

Two miles south of Fort Bragg, the **Mendocino Coast Botanical Gardens** extend down to the Pacific Ocean preserving the native flora in a variety of habitats. Every year this is the idyllic site for Winesong, Mendocino Coast's annual charity fundraiser.

Anderson Valley

This remote valley is arguably one of the most beautiful wine country landscapes in California. It has long been a source of fruit to some of the best wineries in the state, particularly for Pinot Noir and Chardonnay, but in recent years a number of wineries have been established in the valley making estate wines of the very highest quality.

Pinot Noir harvest in the vineyards of Anderson Valley's Goldeneye, owned by Napa's Duckhorn Winery

Grapes have been grown here for decades but it was Dr Donald Edmeades who kick-started the modern era of viticulture in 1964 when he planted 24 acres of premium grape vines. **Edmeades Winery** is now part of the huge Jess Jackson wine empire. The Husch family soon followed and built the first winery in the valley in 1971. This still retains its rustic character although ownership changed several years ago. Next to come along was Ted Bennett, who left his audio business in the San Francisco Bay area to establish **Navarro Vineyards** in 1974. Like many of the valley's wineries, Navarro produces Pinot Noir, Riesling and Gewürztraminer, and while Pinot Noir is the king of the valley, Alsatian varietals are a close second.

When other French champagne houses were setting up shop in Napa Valley, the great champagne house **Roederer** moved into the Anderson Valley in 1982. The head of

Navarro Vineyards in Anderson Valley specialize in Pinot Noir and Alsatian grape varieties

Roederer spent several years searching California for the ideal site and decided that Anderson Valley provided just the right cool climate and well-drained soil for the Roederer style. The proof, as they say, is in the pudding and what delicious pudding it is.

These were pioneering years for Mendocino County. In that same year—1982—Milla Handley made her first Chardonnay in her cellar at home. Thirty years later she makes her wines at **Handley Cellars**, one of the more prominent wineries in the area.

In the following years, the wine business hasn't exactly exploded but the number of outstanding wineries has more than doubled. Napa's **Duckhorn Winery** entered the arena with Goldeneye, which produces several different bottlings of wonderful Pinot Noir, but most of the wineries are small, family affairs. **Londer**, **Breggo** and **Esterlina** are all wineries to watch.

Yorkville Highlands

This recently designated AVA, just to the south of

Boonville, has few wineries of any interest. **Maple Creek Winery** lies at the end of a long, steep driveway and is the dream of Tom Rodrigues and Linda Stutz. Apart from several interesting wines the tasting room also displays Tom's paintings. He is a prominent baseball artist and his best-known work in the wine industry is his label design for Far Niente, the celebrated Napa winery.

Hopland

Back inland, Hopland sits firmly on Highway 101 and as the name suggests this was once the center of a thriving hop industry.

Mendocino Brewing Company started here before moving to larger premises in Ukiah to the north, the county seat. Grapes have replaced hops and the Fetzer family became the biggest player in town. Their **Valley Oaks Center** was an ambitious celebration of food and wine complete with deluxe guest rooms and a remarkable organic garden before organic was trendy. Sadly, it closed in 2006 after Fetzer sold their winery to the Brown Forman group. It has been reincarnated as **Campovida** after it was taken over by Magnanimus Wine Group, which produces organic and biodynamic Mendocino wines. The 50-acre property is being restored to its former glory although it will only be open from Thursday through Sunday.

Paul Dolan was the farsighted winemaker who established Fetzer as a leader in the organic wine movement. He produced wines that were well balanced, exhibiting distinct varietal characteristics with 100 percent organic fruit at a time when organic agriculture was still considered eccentric. Paul Dolan still pursues his organic passion at **Parducci Wine Cellars**, a long-established winery that he purchased with partners in the mid-1990s. It is the first carbon-neutral winery in America and is promoted as America's Greenest Winery.

The Fetzer family has moved into other wine ventures and Danny Fetzer opened **Jeriko Estate Winery** just to the north of town in 1999. In the true Fetzer tradition both organic and biodynamic farming methods are used.

Hopland has become a hotbed of environmentalism and apart from the proliferation of organic-grape farmers, the town is home to the **Solar Living Institute**, dedicated to promoting sustainable living through inspirational environmental education.

The wines produced in this heartland of Mendocino never reach the quality of those from Anderson Valley, but you would be hard pressed to find a more hardcore group of winemakers dedicated to sustainable and ecologically sound farming practices.

Redwood Valley

The pinnacle of this movement is hidden in the remote Redwood Valley a few miles north of Ukiah. In a classic 1960s tale, Paul and Beba Frey moved from New York to this rural isolation to raise their 12 children in a completely natural environment. In 1980 the children, now adults, decided to enter the wine industry, but on their terms. They created the first organic winery in America and in 1996 became the US's first producer of certified biodynamic wines. Not only is the fruit organic but so are the wines, one of only a tiny handful of wineries where absolutely no sulfites are used. A common

Anderson Valley's more functional tasting rooms are a world away from Napa Valley's glitz

criticism is that the process has become more important than the end result and the quality of Frey's wines can be erratic but you have to admire the dedication to their idealistic principles. The winery itself is straight from the Sixties; an eccentric and whimsical collection of wooden buildings inhabited by an enormous extended family with children, dogs and cats everywhere.

Mendocino is a magnet for eccentrics. Just outside Ukiah is an alembic brandy distillery producing what has been described as the world's best liquor using 19th century hand methods on an antique cognac still. In 1981, a tattooed Hubert Germain-Robin was hitchhiking up Highway 101 and was picked up by Ansley Coale. Coale heard Germain-Robin's sad tale of his centuries-old family distillery in Cognac being taken over by the giant Martell. The following year, **Germain-Robin** found an antique still at an abandoned cognac distillery and had it shipped to Coale's ranch in Ukiah. Instead of using the thin, high-acid wines traditionally used for

The Anderson Valley Pinot Noir Festival is held every May

cognac they decided to use premium wines such as Pinot Noir. **The New York Times** hailed the results as "far better brandies than he or his ancestors ever made in France. The depth and richness of the XO are extraordinary."

WINERIES & MORE

Pacific Star Winery
3300 North Highway 1
Ft Bragg, CA 95437
Tel: 707 964 1155
www.pacificstarwinery.com
Twelve miles north of Ft Bragg—mile marker 73.58.
Open daily 11AM–5PM.

Husch Vineyards Winery & Tasting Room
4400 Highway 128

Philo, CA 95466
Tel: 800 554 8724
www.huschvineyards.com
Open daily 10AM–5PM.

Navarro Vineyards
5601 Highway 128
Philo, CA 95466
Tel: 707 895 3686
www.navarrowine.com
Open daily 10AM–5PM.

Roederer Estate
4501 Highway 128
Philo, CA 95466
Tel: 707 895 2288
www.roedererestate.com
Open daily 11AM–5PM.

Handley Cellars
3151 Highway 128
Philo, CA 95466
Tel: 707 895 3876
www.handleycellars.com
Open daily 10AM–5PM.

**Londer Vineyards
Tasting Room**
14051 Highway 128
Boonville, CA 95415
Tel: 707 895 3900
www.londervineyards.com
Open Thurs-Mon
11AM–5PM.

Breggo Cellars
11001 Highway 128
Boonville, CA 95415
Tel: 707 895 9589
www.breggo.com
Open daily 11AM–5PM.

**Esterlina Vineyards
& Winery**
1200 Holmes Ranch Road
PO Box 2
Philo, CA 95466
Tel: 707 895 2920
Open by appointment
only.

Parducci Wine Cellars
501 Parducci Road
Ukiah, CA 95482
Tel: 888 362 9463
www.parducci.com
Open daily 10AM–5PM.

**Jeriko Estate Winery
Estate House and
Tasting Room**
12148 Hewlitt and
Sturtevant Road
(off Route 101)
Hopland, CA 95449
Tel: 707 744 1140
www.jeriko.us

Open daily
10AM–5PM (summer),
11AM–4PM (winter).

Germain-Robin
PO Box 1059
Ukiah, CA 95482
Tel: 800 782 8145
www.germain-robin.com
Visits strictly by
appointment.

Maple Creek Winery
20799 Highway 128
Yorkville, CA 95494
Tel: 707 895 3001
www.maplecreekwine.com
Open daily 10:30AM–5PM
(hours may be shorter in
winter).

ATTRACTIONS
Skunk Train
100 West Laurel Street
Fort Bragg, CA 95437-3410
Tel: 707 964 6371
www.skunktrain.com

**Mendocino Coast
Botanical Gardens**
18220 North Highway 1
Fort Bragg, CA 95437-8773
Tel: 707 964 4352
www.gardenbythesea.org

Solar Living Institute
13771 South Highway 101
Hopland, CA 95449
Tel: 707 472 2450
www.solarliving.org
Open Mon-Fri 9AM–5PM.

Lake County

Clear Lake is the largest natural lake in California and possibly the oldest lake on the continent. It's the main reason most people visit this remote corner of wine country. Wine is almost an afterthought. Water sports, hiking, gambling and a host of outdoor activities take precedence. You won't find the glamorous lifestyle of Napa here. The atmosphere is much more down-to-earth and a Country and Western concert is likely to be far more popular than an art gallery opening.

Although vines were planted here as far back as 1870, Prohibition put a temporary end to the industry and it wasn't until the 1960s that a few visionary growers realized the county's potential. In 1965 there were 100 acres under vine: today there are over 9,000 acres and rising. The legendary grape grower Andy Beckstoffer, who owns many of the most valuable vineyards in Napa Valley, has owned three Cabernet Sauvignon vineyards here since the 1990s and major players including Beringer, Kendall Jackson and Louis

Martini, which all own Lake County vineyards. As the price of good vineyard land continues to escalate, growers are increasingly looking for bargains and there is no doubt that this volcanic land around Clear Lake produces first-class fruit. The quality of the fruit has made it very desirable and most of it is shipped out of Lake County to Napa and Sonoma.

British music hall star Lily Langtry lived in this house in her vineyards near Clearlake. She was once mistress of the future King Edward VII of England

Until recently there were few wineries of note here and today there are still only 22 wineries in total but this number is gradually growing. There isn't the capacity required to process anywhere near all the fruit grown here and even some of the biggest wineries in Lake County have to use custom crush facilities to the south.

HOW TO GET TO LAKE COUNTY

Lake County is remote and there is no fast way to get there; it's at least a two-hour drive from San Francisco. Highway 29 climbs from Calistoga up past Mount St Helena and drops down to Middletown at the southern end of the county. The alternative is to drive north on Highway

LANGTRY ESTATE AND VINEYARDS

101 to the Highway 175 exit in Hopland. Lake County is remote however you look at it.

This is seismic California. A 4,300-foot dormant volcano, Mount Konocti, dominates the landscape and is responsible for the mineral-rich and well-drained soil of the region. Most of the vineyards are above 1,400 feet and can be as high as 3,000 feet and this is the northernmost corner of the North Coast AVA. The vines that seem to prosper here are Bordeaux varietals, particularly reds. Many other varietals are planted though they don't always produce the best quality wines.

Lake County wineries

Langtry Estate and Vineyards is both the oldest and largest winegrower in Lake County. Lily Langtry was a famous British actress who started making wine here in 1888 and her original home is still on the property. This is the closest winery to Napa Valley, near Middletown at the southern end of Lake County. Orville Magoon revived the winery over 40

sive marketing, Brassfield Estate has become one of the most recognized wineries in the area.

The High Valley AVA is home to a cluster of wineries in addition to Brassfield. The other concentration of wineries is around Kelseyville on the opposite side of Clear Lake. There are several smaller wineries spread throughout five AVAs, several in spectacular settings.

FOR FURTHER INFORMATION

Log onto
www.lakecountywinegrape.org

WINERIES & MORE

years ago and marketed his wines under the Guenoc label. He sold his interest in the company in 2003.

Jerry Brassfield started buying land in the High Valley AVA on the eastern shore of Clear Lake in 1973 and continued to acquire land until he owned both the east and west sections of High Valley including Round Mountain Volcano. In 1998 he established **Brassfield Estate Winery**. There are 19 grape varieties grown on 350 acres of land and all of Brassfield's wines are estate grown and bottled. Through aggres-

Langtry Estate and Vineyards

21000 Butts Canyon Road
Middletown, CA 95461
Tel: 707 987 2385
www.langtryestate.com
Open daily 11AM–5PM.

Brassfield Estate Winery

10915 High Valley Road
Clearlake Oaks, CA 95423
Tel: 707 998 1895
www.brassfieldestate.com
Open daily 10AM–5PM
(summer),
Mon-Fri 10AM–5PM
(winter).

WHERE TO STAY AND EAT

Mendocino

ACCOMODATIONS
Brewery Gulch Inn
9401 Coast Highway
1 North
Mendocino, CA 95460
Tel: 800 578 4454
www.brewerygulchinn.com

Joshua Grindle Inn
44800 Little Lake Road
Mendocino, CA 95460
Tel: 707 937 4143
www.joshuagrindleinn.com

Little River Inn
7901 North Highway 1
Little River, CA 95456
Tel: 707 937 5942
www.littleriverinn.com

Stanford Inn by the Sea
Highway 1 and Comptche
Ukiah Road
Mendocino, CA 95460
Tel: 707 937 5615
www.stanfordinn.com

RESTAURANT
Café Beaujolais
961 Ukiah Street
Mendocino, CA 95460
Tel: 707 937 5614
www.cafebeaujolais.com

Boonville

ACCOMODATIONS
**Boonville Hotel
and Restaurant**
14050 Highway 128
Boonville, CA 95415
Tel: 707 895 2210
www.boonvillehotel.com

Anderson Valley vineyards supply fruit to wineries throughout California

The quaint town of Mendocino juts out over the Pacific Ocean

RESTAURANT
Boonville Hotel
Restaurant
14050 Highway 128
Boonville CA 95415
Tel: 707 895 2210
California cuisine

Hopland

ACCOMODATIONS
Hopland Inn
13401 S. Highway 101
Hopland, CA 95449
Tel: 707 744 1890
www.hoplandinn.com

RESTAURANT
Bluebird Café
13340 S. Highway 101
Hopland, CA 95449

Tel: 707 744 1633
American diner

Lakeport

ACCOMODATIONS
Lakeport English Inn
675 North Main Street
Lakeport, CA 95453
Tel: 707 263 4317
www.lakeportenglishinn.com

Knocoti Harbor Resort
8727 Soda Bay Road
Kelseyville, CA 95451
Tel: 707 279 4281
www.knocotiharbor.com

SAN FRANCISCO

S AN FRANCISCO is the American city *par excellence*. It is small, just 49 square miles in area, with good public transportation, a temperate climate, world-class museums, charming city parks, the biggest Chinatown outside of China, enough hotel rooms to suit every pocket and taste and a vibrant dining scene. Add to this a spectacular setting and what more could you want. Only the occasional earthquake is likely to shake things up!

It is a great city to walk around in, as the scale is more human than many of the huge American metropolises, but just remember that summers in San Francisco can be decidedly chilly. High temperatures in California's Central Valley suck cool air in through the Golden Gate—the same cool air that allows Pinot Noir to flourish—and a blanket of fog can keep the city blanketed for days. It is often described as nature's air conditioning, and as Mark Twain is famously supposed to have said, "The coldest winter I ever spent was a summer in San Francisco."

The city is surrounded by wine country: to the north, to the east and to the south. To the west is the Pacific Ocean that creates the climate that makes it all possible. This is undeniably one of the world's great tourist destinations and worthy of a visit in its own right but as a base for wine country exploration it is unsurpassed.

The highlight of the city for anyone interested in food and wine is the **Ferry Building Marketplace** located inside San Francisco's historic Ferry Building, which was built in 1898 and survived the 1906 earthquake. A farmer's market is held here every Tuesday, Thursday and Saturday but it is the vibrant retail scene inside the building that will whet any gourmet's appetite. Several artisan producers sell their products here, including Cowgirl Creamery (see page 201), McEvoy Ranch Olive Oil and Hog Island Oysters.

《 The vineyards of Thomas Fogarty sit high above Silicon Valley, a few miles south of San Francisco

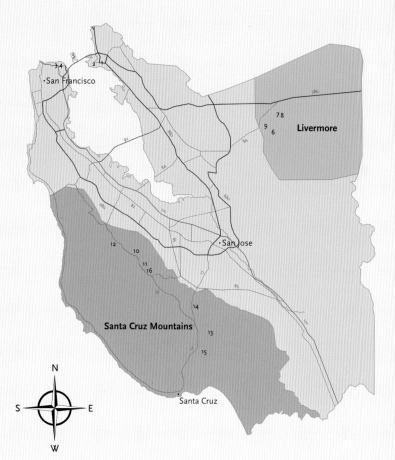

San Francisco

1. Rosenblum Cellars
2. Rock Wall Wines
3. Wattle Creek
4. Winery Collective
5. The Winery

Livermore

6. Wente Vineyards
7. Concannon Vineyard
8. La Rochelle/Steven Kent Winery
9. Thomas Coyne Wines

Santa Cruz Mountains

10. Ridge Vineyards
11. Mount Eden Winery
12. Thomas Fogarty Winery
13. Burrell School Vineyards and Winery
14. Testarossa Vineyards
15. Wines of Vine Hill
16. Savannah-Chanelle Vineyards

WINE LABELS TO LOOK FOR IN SAN FRANCISCO

RIDGE 2008
MONTE BELLO®

MONTE BELLO ESTATE VINEYARD
72% CABERNET SAUVIGNON, 28% MERLOT
SANTA CRUZ MOUNTAINS   13.3% ALCOHOL BY VOLUME
GROWN, PRODUCED & BOTTLED BY RIDGE VINEYARDS
18100 MONTE BELLO RD, BOX 1810, CUPERTINO, CALIFORNIA 95015

2008
Thomas Fogarty
SANTA CRUZ MOUNTAINS
PINOT NOIR

the **Whip**
2009
WHITE WINE
43% SEMILLON, 21% SAUVIGNON BLANC,
21% VIOGNIER, 7% MUSCAT CANELLI,
5% GEWURZTRAMINER, 3% ORANGE MUSCAT
LIVERMORE VALLEY

WENTE
VINEYARDS
ESTATE GROWN
Charles Wetmore

CABERNET SAUVIGNON
LIVERMORE VALLEY
SAN FRANCISCO BAY

2009.
TESTAROSSA
CHARDONNAY
SANTA LUCIA HIGHLANDS
ROSELLA'S VINEYARD

In downtown Los Gatos, Testarossa Winery occupies the historic Noviate Winery, the fourth oldest continuously operating winery in California

Restaurants, coffee bars and a first-class wine merchant make this a destination in its own right.

There are no wineries within the city limits, but there is no shortage of wine bars and even a couple of winery tasting rooms. However, a short drive across the Bay Bridge, in Alameda, an old naval base has become the center for urban winemaking.

Kent Rosenblum produces some of the finest Zinfandels in California and established Alameda as a serious winemaking

center when he moved **Rosenblum Cellars** to its present location in 1987. He sold the winery to the mighty Diageo conglomerate in 2008 but he continues to consult for them. His daughter Shauna is continuing the family tradition at **Rock Wall Wines** just a stone's throw away in an old naval hanger. Several other boutique wineries, known as the **Alameda Point Vintners**, operate from here and their wines are available for tasting at the Rock Wall Wine Company.

Even if you don't have time for the one-hour drive to Napa, Sonoma, Livermore or the Santa Cruz mountains, you can hop onto a ferry at **San Francisco's Ferry Plaza**, stop to grab a gourmet picnic and within 20 minutes be at Rosenblum Cellars. Don't expect to see any vineyards—this is urban industrial winemaking and it definitely lacks charm. All the fruit is shipped in from the finest vineyards throughout California and the wines made here are the equal of any you are likely to taste anywhere. An even closer winery has opened on Treasure Island. The Bay Bridge, not to be confused with the Golden Gate Bridge, is 4.5 miles long and the first span crosses to Yerba Buena Island, to which Treasure Island is attached. Treasure Island was created for the Golden Gate International Exposition in 1939, from fill dredged up from the San Francisco Bay. During World War II the island became a naval base and remained so until 1997. The old navy buildings are now used for everything from affordable housing to movie sound stages and even a winery. Simply called **The Winery**, it is the first fully operating winery within the city of San Francisco and although

the primary purpose appears to be as an event space, winemaker Bryan Kane—who founded Vie Winery in Lake County, which makes Rhône varietals and Zinfandel—is serious about his wine. He sources fruit from some of the best vineyards in Napa and Sonoma. The facilities opened in September 2010 and it will be interesting to see what transpires.

WINERIES & MORE

Rosenblum Cellars
2900 Main Street
Alameda, CA 94501
Tel: 510 865 7007
www.rosenblumcellars.com
Open daily 11AM–6PM.

Rock Wall Wines
2301 Monarch Street,
Suite 300
Alameda, CA 94501
Tel: 510 522 5700
www.rockwallwines.com
Open Thurs-Sun
12PM-6PM.

Wattle Creek
900 North Point Street
San Francisco, CA 94109
Tel: 415 358 1206
www.wattlecreek.com
Open Mon-Sat 11AM–9PM,
Sun 11AM–7PM.

SAN FRANCISCO

1. Joie de Vivre Hospitality
2. Kimpton Hotel Group
3. The Clift Hotel
4. The Fairmont
5. The Huntington Hotel
6. Taj Campton Place
7. Westin St. Francis
8. Boulevard
9. Farallon
10. La Folie
11. Restaurant Gary Danko
12. RN74
13. Spruce

Winery Collective
485 Jefferson Street
San Francisco, CA 94109
Tel: 415 929 9463
www.winerycollective.com
Open daily 11AM–9PM.

The Winery
200 California Avenue
Building 180 North
San Francisco, CA 94130
Tel: 415 735 8423
www.winery-sf.com
Open by appointment.

Livermore

Drive out of San Francisco for about 45 minutes along Highway 580 toward Lodi and the Sierra Nevada to Livermore, a city perhaps best know as the home of the Lawrence Livermore National Laboratory, the premier research and development institution for science and technology applied to national security. This suburban sprawl appears to be the most unlikely setting for viticulture but drive on for just a couple of miles southeast of the freeway and enter into a land of vineyards and wineries. Just don't expect the picturesque landscape of the rest of California's wine country.

Grapes were first planted here in the 1840s and by Prohibition there were over 50 wineries in the region. This was perfect terroir with poor, rocky soil, hot days and cool nights with cooling air coming into the east-west valley from the San Francisco Bay, which created a 30° F temperature drop during the growing season. This was an area producing bulk fruit for jug wines but in recent years this policy has changed

Wente Vineyards is the biggest producer in Livermore

with the need to make quality wines at reasonable prices to compete with other appellations. Development consumed a lot of the vineyard land and today most of the wineries line Tesla Road.

Wente Vineyards is by far the biggest player with over one million cases produced annually. Many of the wines are lackluster

and a high percentage go to export but they produce a Chardonnay that regularly receives critical acclaim and several small lot wines that are created specifically for members of the Wente Vineyards Wine Club. What most of the wines lack in quality is more than made up for by a tasting room experience that includes a white-table-cloth dining room serving exceptionally good food, a summer concert series with performers as high profile as Willie Nelson and Liza Minnelli and even an 18-hole championship golf course designed by Greg Norman. CH Wente established the winery in 1883 and it's still run by the Wente family.

Concannon Vineyard was established in the same year as Wente, in 1883, and remains a family-run operation. Concannon's major claim to fame is the introduction of the much-maligned Petite Syrah to California and this has become their flagship wine. They also make many other varietals, many of which would have been better left alone.

Also on Tesla road is a winery that is completely incongruous in that it specializes in Pinot Noir and this is certainly not Pinot country. They produce some of the very best wines coming out of Livermore albeit from fruit that is sourced from Oregon down to Arroyo Seco. **La Rochelle Winery** is the enterprise of Steven Mirassou. In 1854 the Mirassou family established their eponymous winery in what is now Silicon Valley near San José. The wines were never particularly interesting and, appropriately, the brand was sold to industry giant Gallo in 2003. Increasing competition in the wine industry has resulted in many scions of the old wine families taking the quality of their wines to a whole new level. Gina Gallo is a textbook example of this trend. Sixth generation Steven Mirassou is another, taking the family winemaking

tradition to levels unimaginable to his ancestors. When he couldn't negotiate the extension of a lease on the family's original winery location he moved out to Livermore.

Steven Kent Winery shares the same premises as La Rochelle for the obvious reason that this too is owned by Steven Mirassou. Steven Kent wines have a dedicated following almost on a cult level. Small lot, carefully crafted wines are made in a classic California style with lots of fruit and intense flavors. If you enjoy this big, bold style of winemaking, you won't be disappointed.

Some distance away from Tesla Road, **Thomas Coyne** moved his winery into an 1881 building originally occupied by Chateau Bellevue Winery. At the end of a long dirt road a group of sagging wooden buildings from the old winery forms a picturesque backdrop for picnics with a bottle of Coyne's wine. The grapes are sourced from vineyards in the Gold Country, Contra Costa County as well as Livermore and the results, particularly the Rhône-style wines, generally represent excellent value.

WINERIES & MORE

Wente Vineyards
5050 Arroyo Road
Livermore, CA 94550
Tel: 925 456 2300
www.wentevineyards.com
Open daily 11AM–6:30PM.

Concannon Vineyard
4590 Tesla Road
Livermore, CA 94550
Tel: 800 258 9866
www.concannonvineyard.com
Open daily 11AM–4:30PM.

**La Rochelle/
Steven Kent Winery**
5443 Tesla Road
Livermore, CA 94550
Tel: 925 243 6442
www.lrwine.com
www.stevenkent.com
Open daily 12PM–4PM.

Thomas Coyne Wines
51 East Vallecitos Road
Livermore, CA 94550
Tel: 925 373 6541
thomascoynewinery.com
Open weekends only
12PM–5PM.

Santa Cruz Mountains

Just 90 minutes south of San Francisco the Santa Cruz Mountains rise above San José, the second biggest city in California. This is the center of the world's technology industry, home to Apple, Hewlett Packard and Intel as well as eBay and Google. Only a few miles away the landscape changes from concrete and glass office parks to steep, redwood-forested hillsides. Winegrowing in these mountains dates back to the 1860s and an increasing number of escapees from the hi-tech world are setting up shop as winery owners. From San Francisco take either Highway 101 or Highway 280, which is by far the more scenic drive, to Highway 85 to Highway 17.

In most of California's premium wine-growing areas the climate is controlled by the Pacific Ocean and the majority of vineyards in the San Cruz Mountains are only 15 miles away from the coast. This is a region of long, fog-free days with few heat spikes, enabling fruit to ripen slowly, and an ample winter rainfall allows many vineyards to be dry-farmed. Pinot Noir and Chardonnay both thrive here but small production has limited the public exposure this AVA receives. Today, the area is frequently overlooked as a wine region

and it's easy to understand why. The wineries and vineyards are hidden along steep mountain roads that are often so winding that getting lost is almost inevitable. You can drive over the mountains on Highway 17 from San José to Santa Cruz without seeing a single vine.

The irony of this oversight is that the Santa Cruz Mountains AVA is home to two of California's greatest wineries.

Ridge Vineyards sits at an elevation of appropriately 2,600 feet on a high ridge overlooking the city of San José and Silicon Valley. Their Monte Bello Cabernet Sauvignon has consistently been one of the best red wines produced in the state for over 40 years. The winery dates back to 1885 when Dr Osea Perrone bought 180 acres of land near the top of Monte Bello Ridge and released the wine under that name in 1892. New owners in the 1960s expanded the production to included several other varietals, most notably Zinfandel which has become one of their signature wines. The modern success of Ridge is largely due to the winemaking talents of Paul Draper, who is a 40-year veteran of the winery.

Mount Eden Vineyards is similarly located 2,000 feet up on poor, mountain topsoil whose low-yield vineyards consistently produce fruit of great intensity and character. The legendary winemaker Martin Ray planted six acres of Chardonnay vines from Burgundian stock in the early 1940s and although the plot has increased to 20 acres, the yield is so small, averaging less than two tons per acre, far less than most California Chardonnay vineyards, that fewer than 2,000 cases are produced annually. Mount Eden was one of the first boutique wineries and the Mount Eden Estate Chardonnay is one of the longest continuous estate-bottled productions in North America.

Several other notable wineries, often with sweeping views, punctuate the mountains. **Thomas Fogarty Winery** is notable both for its views and an excellent range of vineyard designate Pinot Noir and Chardonnay. **Burrell**

<< Racking barrels of single vineyard Pinot Noir at Testarossa Winery. The process involves transferring the wine while leaving the sediment behind

School is perhaps the most whimsical, housed in an old school building with wonderful views over Chardonnay vineyards to the Pacific coast. If only the wines were as delightful as the location!

The vineyards at **Vine Hill Winery**, tucked away far from sight, have been producing good fruit since the late 1800s. Most of the vines were Zinfandel but David Bruce, one of the new pioneers in the region, replaced Zinfandel with Pinot Noir vines. Sal Godinez, the winemaker, is one of the great California wine industry success stories. He came originally from Mexico to work as a gardener at Freemark Abbey Winery in Napa and after 15 months a cellar opening became available. Sal eventually moved to Saintsbury in Carneros, where he learned the art of making first-class Pinot Noir. In 2005 he became winemaker at Vine Hill, producing some of the best Pinot in the area.

At the foot of the mountains, in the charming and exclusive town of Los Gatos, just past the Ferrari and Bentley dealership, the old 19th-century, stone **Novitiate Winery** has been transformed into a modern gravity-flow facility producing several highly acclaimed vineyard designate Pinot Noirs. **The Testarossa Winery** sources fruit from many different regions of California and in addition to the wines, both its historic building and proximity to Highway 17 in downtown Los Gatos make it well worth a visit.

Saratoga is another exclusive little town a short distance from Los Gatos. It nestles right at the foot of the Santa Cruz Mountains and **Savannah-Chanelle Vineyards** is a four-mile drive up the winding road above the town. The winery was established in 1892 and has been through multiple ownerships, most recently under the name Congress Springs, until the Ballard family purchased the property in 1996. They named the winery after their two daughters. Winemaker Tony Craig, a Brit who came from David Bruce Winery, specializes in Pinot Noir, often in the big, fruit-forward Californian style.

After a day wine tasting and negotiating winding roads, what could be more appropriate than a short drive down Highway 17 to

A MOUNTAIN VINEYARD, SANTA CRUZ

the seaside town of Santa Cruz and a ride on the old wooden rollercoaster at the beach boardwalk?

WINERIES & MORE

Ridge Vineyards
17100 Monte Bello Road
Cupertino, CA 95014
Tel: 408 867 3233
www.ridgewine.com
Open Sat and Sun
11AM–5PM Apr-Oct,
11AM–4PM Nov-Mar.

Mount Eden Winery
22020 Mount Eden Road
Saratoga, CA 95070
Tel: 888 865 9463
www.mounteden.com
No tasting. For tour
reservations call
408 867 5832 Ext 10.

Thomas Fogarty Winery
19501 Skyline Boulevard
Woodside, CA 94602
Tel: 650 851 6777
www.fogartywinery.com
Open Wed-Sun 11AM–5PM.

**Burrell School
Vineyards and Winery**
24060 Summit Road
Los Gatos, CA 95033
Tel: 408 353 6290
www.burrellschool.com
Open Thur-Sun 11AM–5PM.

Testarossa Vineyards
300A College Avenue
Los Gatos, CA 95030
Tel: 408 354 6150
www.testarossa.com
Open daily 11AM–5PM
except major holidays.

Wines of Vine Hill
2300 Jarvis Road
Santa Cruz, CA 95065
Tel: 831 427 0436
www.winesofvinehill.com
By appointment only.

**Savannah-Chanelle
Vineyards**
23600 Big Basin Way
Saratoga, CA 95070
Tel: 408 741 2934
www.savannahchanelle.com
Open daily 11AM-5PM.

WHERE TO STAY AND EAT

Within the scope of this book it's impossible to provide a comprehensive listing for one of the world's major international tourist destinations that also happens to be a culinary mecca. The hotel listings represent some of the hotels in the best locations that maintain a very high standard.

ACCOMODATIONS

These are two boutique hotel chains that originated in San Francisco. Both have several properties throughout the city:

Joie de Vivre Hospitality
530 Bush Street, Suite 501
San Francisco, CA 94108
Tel: 510 986 8049
www.jdvhotels.com

Kimpton Hotel Group
222 Kearny Street
San Francisco, CA 94108
Tel: 415 397 5572
www.kimptonhotels.com

CLASSIC SAN FRANCISCO HOTELS INCLUDE:

The Clift Hotel
495 Geary Street
San Francisco, CA 94102
Tel: 415 775 4700
www.clifthotel.com

The Fairmont
950 Mason Street
San Francisco, CA 94108
Tel: 415 772 5000
www.fairmont.com/
sanfrancisco

Gourmet Ghetto is the nickname of the business district in the city of Berkeley, California, and is home to endless epicurean delights

The Huntington Hotel
1075 California Street
San Francisco, CA 94108
Tel: 415 474 5400
www.huntingtonhotel.com

Taj Campton Place
340 Stockton Street
San Francisco, CA 94108
Tel: 415 781 5555
www.tajhotels.com

Westin St Francis
335 Powell Street
San Francisco, CA 94103
Tel: 415 397 7000
www.westinstfrancisco.com

RESTAURANTS
This sampling of a few of
San Francisco's outstand-
ing restaurants highlights
establishments that have
a wide range of California
wines, wines by the glass,
wine pairing menus and a
sommelier:

Boulevard
1 Mission Street
San Francisco, CA 94105
Tel: 415 543 6084
www.boulevardrestaurant.com
Californian/French

Farallon
450 Post Street
San Francisco, CA 94102
Tel: 415 956 6969
www.farallon.com
Seafood

La Folie
2316 Polk Street
San Francisco, CA 94109
Tel: 415 776 5577
www.lafolie.com
French

Restaurant Gary Danko
800 North Point Street
San Francisco, CA 94109
Tel: 415 749 2060
www.garydanko.com
Californian/French

RN74
301 Mission Street
San Francisco, CA 94105
Tel: 415 543 7474
www.michaelmina.net/rn74

Spruce
3640 Sacramento Street
San Francisco, CA 94118
Tel: 415 931 5100
www.sprucesf.com

CENTRAL COAST

NAPA AND SONOMA are not the be-all and end-all of quality California wine production. The 400-mile drive down Highway 101 between San Francisco and Los Angeles follows the historic Camino Real and the chain of missions built by Father Junipero Serra over 200 years ago. The missionaries brought vines to California and although this area has been slow to establish a reputation for quality the last ten years have seen a dramatic improvement. The movie *Sideways* has done more than anything to put the Central Coast on the popular wine map.

The region is home to several AVAs from the Santa Cruz Mountains down to the Santa Rita Hills near Santa Barbara, all producing fruit of the highest quality. Viticultural techniques have improved dramatically over the past few years and the better fruit combined with improvements in winemaking have resulted in wines that are the equal of any in the New World, particularly Pinot Noir, Chardonnay and Rhône blends. Central Coast fruit is used by many Napa and Sonoma wineries both for their high-end vineyard-designate wines and for second-label bottlings.

If the lure of good wine is not enough then how about the abundance of visitor attractions that range from spectacular scenery to quaint villages to castles? The legendary scenic drive down Big Sur from Monterey to San Luis Obispo on Highway 1 alone makes the journey worthwhile and a short distance inland, vineyards stretch for miles. This is California at its best and instead of flying between Los Angeles and San Francisco, why not take a leisurely three-day drive and spend time visiting some of the wineries on the way?

《 Beneath Eberle Winery in East Paso Robles. The winery organizes tours of its 16,000 square feet of underground caves

Monterey County

1. Talbott Vineyards
2. Bernadus Winery
3. Château Julien
4. Chalone Vineyard
5. Galante Vineyards
6. Scheid Vineyards
7. Ventana Vineyards
8. A Taste of Monterey

Paso Robles

9. Justin Vineyards and Winery
10. Tablas Creek
11. Opolo Vineyards
12. Windward Vineyard
13. L'Aventure Winery
14. Calcareous Vineyard
15. Whalebone Vineyard
16. Adelaida Cellars
17. Nadeau Family Vintners
18. Peachy Canyon Winery
19. Clautiere Vineyard
20. Eberle Winery
21. J Lohr
22. Chateau Margene

23. Wild Horse Winery
24. Tobin James Cellars
25. Robert Hall Winery

Edna Valley and Arroyo Grande

26. Baileyana Winery Tasting Room
27. Domaine Alfred
28. Saucelito Canyon Winery
29. Claiborne & Churchill Vintners
30. Talley Vineyards
31. Laetitia Vineyard and Winery

WINE LABELS TO LOOK
FOR IN CENTRAL COAST

Family-owned Maloy O'Neill Vineyards in East Paso Robles boasts a chapel-like tasting room

Monterey County

John Steinbeck immortalized Monterey Bay in his classic novel, *Cannery Row*. The canneries have long ceased operation and the old buildings are now home not only to the inevitable T-shirt shops and tourist traps cashing in on the town's colorful heritage but also to one of the world's great aquariums.

The **Monterey Bay Aquarium**'s mission is to inspire conservation of the oceans and it does this through spectacular underwater exhibits and an ongoing educational program encouraging the consumption of sustainable seafood.

Gastronomy extends beyond the aquarium to several wine-tasting venues both in **Cannery Row** and in the neighboring, picture-perfect town of **Carmel-by-**

the-Sea. There is not a vine to be seen in either town but many of the county's wineries have a tasting room presence, easily accessible to the main tourist attractions.

Monterey County is a wine-growing area of two extremes. Most of the vineyards are corporate undertakings dedicated to the production of cheap, bulk wines. They are some of the better bulk wines being produced in California, but they are certainly not wonderful. At the other end of the spectrum are new, small-scale producers, such as Robert Talbott, making wines of great quality and it is on the shirttails of these that many of the bulk producers market their lackluster offerings. To be fair, some of the mass production is of gratifyingly high quality. Jerry Lohr was one of the pioneer growers in Monterey County and although the JLohr label is now usually associated with Paso Robles, much of the fruit for their annual 10-million-case production comes from here. Among wines in the low to medium price range they represent consistently good value.

Monterey County is big—3,300 square miles, with a diverse range of soils and climate that allow vintners to grow a wide variety of grapes. Over 40,000 acres are planted with vines and it's estimated that almost 80 percent of Monterey County fruit is used in Central Coast blends. The region is best known for Chardonnay, which represents over 40 percent of the county's production.

To see the real Monterey wine country take the Carmel Valley Road, which winds through beautiful pastoral mountain landscape until it joins Highway 101 at Greenfield, south of Soledad. Most of the wineries are close to the "Village" (officially Carmel Valley Village), the sleepy commercial hub of the valley 12 miles from Highway 1.

Talbott Vineyards is one of the county's best producers and their small tasting room pours both Chardonnay and Pinot Noir made from fruit grown in Talbott's extensive vineyards in the Santa Lucia Highlands. Talbott's other business as a maker of exquisite ties and shirts has an outlet store across the road with bargains galore for both men and women.

Bernardus Vineyards and Winery is the leading producer in the Carmel Valley, bottling a remarkably good Bordeaux blend called Marinus, made from their estate vineyard. The Bernardus property is a full-scale resort complete

Early morning fog cools the vines at L'Aventure in the Westside hills of Paso Robles

with spa and croquet lawn and is very popular with wedding parties.

The faux château of the **Château Julian Wine Estate** looks impressive but tends to mask the quality of the wines that never seem to quite live up to their grandiose name. The road meanders on for another 35 miles until it joins Highway 101.

The Salinas Valley

Most visitors to Monterey County will want to stay on **Highway 1** and see the major tourist attractions of Monterey, **Carmel** and **Big Sur**. If you do this, you can taste the Monterey wines in several of the tasting rooms scattered around the towns. However, to experience the real wine country you will have to endure the far less interesting drive down Highway 101 through Salinas into the Salinas Valley.

The Salinas Valley is an 85-mile stretch of monotonous landscape with crops punctuated by ugly agricultural towns. The town of Salinas is home to the **National Steinbeck Center**, a modern museum dedicated to the writer, but there is little else of interest.

Vineyards extend across the valley floor as far as the eye can see but these are grapes destined for bulk wines of dubious quality. The good stuff is grown on higher ground and the shining star of the county is the Santa Lucia Highlands sub-appellation. This 18-mile long strip of bench land above the Salinas Valley parallels Highway 101. It is mainly small lot cultivation and the grapes are of such high quality that many of the state's most notable wineries source their fruit from here for single vineyard designate wine. Gary Pisoni grows some of the most sought-after Pinot Noir grapes in America and the prices he can command are appropriately astronomical. Wines made from Pisoni fruit are often criticized for being too big with high alcohol and lacking in subtlety and finesse. Gary Pisoni is one of the great personalities of the California wine industry and in many ways the wines made from his fruit reflect the personality of the grower.

Chalone

High in the Gavilan Mountains opposite the Santa Lucia Highlands, above Soledad, lies Chalone AVA, which exists solely because of **Chalone Vineyards**. The drive from Soledad through a barren, brown landscape changes dramatically after climbing to 1,600 feet and suddenly entering lush, green vineyards. Most of the land is planted with Chardonnay and the remaining third with Pinot Noir. Both of these Burgundian varietals excel in the limestone-rich soil.

Mount Harlan AVA is perhaps the most obscure and remote in California, but consistently produces some of the state's greatest wines. Josh Jensen spent years poring over geological survey maps looking for the right limestone that would replicate the soils of Burgundy. He found it on top of the Gavilan Mountains, a short distance from Chalone as the crow flies but, by road, a long drive on a remote but beautiful byway along the San Andreas Fault south of Hollister. Even native Californians would have problems identifying it on a map. **The Calera Wine Co** was built in an old limestone processing plant that lent itself to a gravity flow operation. A 30-minute drive up a steep dirt road leads to the spectacular Calera vineyards. How anyone could have the vision to plant vines on this arid mountaintop and turn their fruit into sublime Pinot Noir is almost beyond comprehension.

Calera Wine Co
11300 Cienega Road
Hollister, CA 95023
Tel: 831 637 9170
www.calerawine.com
Open daily 11AM–4:30PM.

WINERIES & MORE

Talbott Vineyards
53 West Carmel Valley Rd
Carmel Valley, CA 93924
Tel: 831 659 3500
www.talbottvineyards.com
Open daily 11AM–5PM.

Bernadus Winery
5 West Carmel Valley Road
Carmel Valley, CA 93924
Tel: 888 648 9463
www.bernadus.com
Open daily 11AM–5PM.

Château Julien
8940 Carmel Valley Road
Carmel, CA 93923
Tel: 805 624 2600
www.chateaujulien.com
Open Mon-Fri 8AM–5PM,
Sat-Sun 11AM–5PM.

Chalone Vineyard
Stonewall Canyon Road
and Highway 146
Soledad, CA 93960
Tel: 831 678 1717
www.chalonevineyard.com
Open Mon-Fri
by appointment,
Sat-Sun 11:30AM–5PM.

Galante Vineyards
Ocean and 7th Avenue
Carmel, CA 93921
Tel: 831 624 3800
www.galantevineyards.com
Open daily 12PM–6PM.

Scheid Vineyards
751 Cannery Row
Monterey, CA 93940
Tel: 831 656 9463
www.scheidvineyards.com
Open daily 11AM–7PM.

Ventana Vineyards
2999 Monterey-Salinas
Highway
Monterey, CA 93940
Tel: 831 372 7415
www.ventanawines.com
Open daily 11AM–5PM.

WINE
VISITORS CENTER

A Taste of Monterey
700 Cannery Row
Monterey, CA 93940
Tel: 831 646 5446
www.tastemonterey.com
Open daily 11AM–6PM.

Paso Robles

Four hours' drive south of San Francisco, Highway 101—the main artery through California's wine country—divides one of the state's fastest-growing wine regions. Paso Robles, which translates as "the pass of the oaks," was a Spanish settlement founded in 1796 with the establishment of Mission San Miguel, a few miles to the north. Vineyards surround the town on every side.

The Paso Robles AVA has two distinct identities, which are separated by the 101 freeway. The eastern section is dominated by high-yield corporate vineyards supplying fruit for Central Coast designate wines. To the west are small artisan wineries producing limited quantities of well-crafted wines with the Paso Robles appellation. There is an inevitable elitism involved here, but the boundaries between the boutique west and commercial east are gradually eroding.

West Paso Robles

West Paso is higher and cooler than the east. The roads that wind through the hilly terrain offer a constantly-changing, bucolic, oak-studded landscape with dozens of small wineries tucked away waiting to be discovered. It's an area that represents wine touring at its best. The wineries differ dramatically in character, from the grandiose exem-

Enjoying a glass of Chardonnay at Chateau Margene as the sun sets over East Paso Robles. The winery also makes superb Cabernets

plified by **Justin Vineyards and Winery**, the self-appointed flagship of West Paso, to much humbler establishments. That the soils here are rich in calcium deposits is suggested by the names of wineries such as **Whalebone** and **Calcareous**, and this factor combined with an ideal growing climate results in some wonderful wines. Particularly notable are the Rhône-style examples that excel in this region. Not far from Justin is **Tablas Creek**, the winery that helped establish West Paso as a serious player in the wine game. The winery is co-owned by the proprietors of Rhône's famed Château Beaucastel.

West Paso is only a few miles from the Pacific Ocean as the crow flies and toward the southern part of the region the Templeton Gap in the Santa Lucia Mountains allows cool air

Mother and daughters sample the wine of Tolo Cellers in Paso Robles

through to blanket the vine-yards, which in turn causes a temperature drop of as much as 40° from summer highs that often reach into the hundreds Fahrenheit. Even the cool-climate grape Pinot Noir is successfully cultivated here and **Wind-ward Vineyard** specializes exclusively in this varietal with great success.

East Paso Robles

East Paso is a different animal. Gone are the hills, winding roads and intimacy of the west. The area is in general flat and hot and, until fairly recently, mass production of mediocre quality fruit was the order of the day. Times have changed and although the large-scale operations are still here, quality has im-proved and wineries such as J Lohr are making wines that represent remarkably good value. The area can be searingly hot in the summer with temperatures in the hundreds but just enough colder air comes in from the coast to cool the nights. Big reds flourish here and Cabernet Sauvi-gnon, Merlot and Zinfan-del do particularly well.

The difference between wines from East Paso and West Paso is still very evi-dent and it's often hard to believe they are even from the same AVA. But changes are happening. **Chateau Margene** on the east side makes superb Cabernet Francs and Cabernet Sauvignons, which are some of the most expensive wines in the whole of the Paso Robles AVA. In West Paso, **Opolo Vineyards** is making very good Cabernets and Merlots from their extensive holdings in East Paso.

Visiting the wineries

Most of the wineries welcome visitors and a few are destinations in their own right. As you would expect, the wineries that focus on wine rather than entertainment tend to produce a better product but nevertheless you can still taste some good wine while having an entertaining visit. In East Paso, **Tobin James** is the happening place. Their Wild West-style tasting room is rocking at weekends and their wine club, with over 18,000 members, is claimed to be the world's biggest. The range of wines made here is encyclopedic and it seems that there isn't a varietal they won't consider making. Not all are great but a few, including Zinfandels, can be remarkably good.

In the **Clautiere Vineyard** tasting room on the east side there always seems to be a party in progress. Costume parties fill the winery calendar and a plentiful supply of theatrical wigs in the tasting room encourages more extroverted visitors to get into the party mood whatever the occasion.

West Paso is more sedate but the barbeques at Opolo Vineyards are justifiably popular. Co-owner Rick Quinn often roasts a whole lamb, reflecting his Croatian heritage, and Opolo's red wines are the perfect accompaniment. At the other end of the spectrum, Justin Vineyards provides elegant dining— a setting more Napa Valley than Paso Robles.

Paso Robles is an area to watch as the quality of its wines continues to improve. The town is improving too with several excellent new restaurants close to the charming town square that provides a focal point for the area. Concerts on the grass are a regular weekend event during the hot summer months. Several of Paso Robles' more remote wineries have opened tasting rooms in downtown allowing the visitor in a hurry to sample a good representative selection of the area's wines without having to stray too far from the freeway.

WINERIES & MORE

WEST PASO

**Justin Vineyards
and Winery**
11680 Chimney Rock Road
Paso Robles, CA 93446
Tel: 805 238 6932
www.justinwine.com
Open daily 10AM–6PM.

Tablas Creek
9339 Adeleida Road
Paso Robles, CA 93446
Tel: 805 238 1231
www.tablascreek.com
Open daily 10AM–5PM.

Opolo Vineyards
7110 Vineyard Drive
Paso Robles, CA 93446
Tel: 805 238 9593
www.opolo.com
Open daily 10AM–5PM.

Windward Vineyard
138 Live Oak Road
Paso Robles, CA 93446
Tel: 805 239 2565
www.windwardvineyard.com
Open daily 10:30AM–5PM.

L'Aventure Winery
2815 Live Oak Road
Paso Robles, CA 93446
Tel: 805 227 1588
www.aventurewine.com
Open Thurs-Sun 11AM–
4PM or by appointment.

Calcareous Vineyard
3430 Peachy Canyon Road
Paso Robles, CA 93446
Tel: 805 239 0289
www.calcareous.com
Open Thurs-Mon
11AM–5PM.

Whalebone Vineyard
8325 Vineyard Drive
Paso Robles, CA 93446
Tel: 805 239 9020
www.whalebonevineyard.com
Open daily 11AM–5PM.

Adelaida Cellars
5805 Adelaida Road
Paso Robles, CA 93446
Tel: 805 239 8980
www.adelaida.com
Open daily 10AM–5PM.

Nadeau Family Vintners
3860 Peachy Canyon Road
Paso Robles, CA 93446
Tel: 805 239 3574
nadeaufamilyvintners.com
Open Fri-Sun 12PM-5PM.

Peachy Canyon Winery
1480 North Bethel Road
Paso Robles, CA 93446
Tel: 805 239 1918
www.peachycanyon.com
Open Daily 11AM–5PM.

EAST PASO

Clautiere Vineyard
1340 Penman Springs Road
Paso Robles, CA 93446
Tel: 805 237 3789

www.clautiere.com
Open daily 12PM-5PM.

Still Waters Vineyards
2750 Old Grove Lane
Paso Robles, CA 93446
Tel: 805 237 9231
www.stillwatersvineyards.com
Open Thurs-Mon
11AM-5PM.

Eberle Winery
3810 Highway 46 East
Paso Robles, CA 93447
Tel: 805 238 9607
www.eberlewinery.com
Open daily 10AM-6PM.

J Lohr
6169 Airport Road
Paso Robles, CA 93446
Tel: 805 239 8900
www.jlohr.com
Open daily 10AM-5PM.

Chateau Margene
4385 La Panza Road
Creston, CA 93432
Tel: 805 238 0421
www.chateaumargene.com
Open Sat-Sun 12PM-6PM.

Wild Horse Winery
1484 Wild Horse
Winery Court
Templeton, CA 93465
Tel: 805 434 2541
www.wildhorsewinery.com
Open daily 11AM-5PM.
Tobin James Cellars
8590 Union Road

Paso Robles, CA 93446
Tel: 805 239 2204
www.tobinjames.com
Open daily 10AM-6PM.

Robert Hall Winery
3443 Mill Road
Paso Robles, CA 93446
Tel: 805 239 1616
www.roberthallwinery.com
Open daily 10AM-6PM.

Edna Valley and Arroyo Grande

San Luis Obispo is a sleepy college town a half hour's drive south of Paso Robles. Vines were originally brought here by missionaries, as they were throughout the California coast, and Father Junipero Serra built his fifth mission here in 1772. **Mission San Luis Obispo de Tolosa** was sold for $510 in 1845 and today it is the historic center of town. It sits by the San Luis Creek and on summer evenings restaurant patios backing onto the creek make the perfect place to sit and savor local cuisine accompanied by Central Coast wines. Every Thursday evening, unless it's raining, a lively farmers' market closes down six blocks of Higuera Street

Laetitia Vineyard & Winery has one of America's largest Pinot Noir vineyards. Here the grapes are harvested for sparkling wines

just one block away from the creek.

A few miles up the coast is the fantastic former home of press baron William Randolph Hearst, **Hearst Castle**, immortalized as Xanadu in Orson Wells' classic film *Citizen Kane*. This is one of the great, must-see sights of California. It is now a state park and tours book up several weeks in advance. The nearby town of **Cambria** is the quintessential seaside arts community filled with galleries and tearooms.

Vineyards less than ten miles from the ocean in West Paso sit as high as 1,500 feet. The vineyards of Edna Valley are only a few hundred feet above sea level and the elevation drop is obvious as Highway 101 falls steeply down to the ocean. There are no mountains to block the maritime air and the weather down here is decidedly cooler than Paso Robles. The twin AVAs of Edna Valley and Arroyo Grande lie nine miles inland from San Luis Obispo, and this cool climate provides one of the longest growing seasons in California, which is ideal for both Chardonnay and Pinot Noir.

The Edna Valley AVA covers only 35 square miles and marine deposits together with volcanic remnants make up soil that gives their wines a distinctive flavor. Arroyo Grande is contiguous with Edna Valley and the terroir is so similar there is virtually no difference in the character of the wines.

The Niven family pioneered grape growing here in the early 1970s and their **Baileyana Winery** tasting room is a jewel of the valley. The Edna Valley farming community built the one-room Independence Schoolhouse in 1909 and the Niven family undertook its restoration in 1998, converting the building into a charming tasting room that retains all the character of the original schoolhouse. It stands surrounded by the Paragon and Firepeak Vineyards.

A short distance down the road **Chamisal** may not have a particularly interesting tasting room but their Pinot Noir is some of the best in the area. The

winery was sold in 2008 to the Crimson Group, owners of Pine Ridge in Napa Valley and Archery Summit in Oregon's Willamette Valley. The wines here can be expected to get even better under the new ownership.

Saucelito Canyon Winery has a small tasting room in the heart of Edna Valley and, unlike most of the Edna Valley and Arroyo Grande wineries, their signature wines are Zinfandels made from old vines grown in a remote corner of the Arroyo Grande Valley. The quality of the wine is consistently high, both subtle and complex, fruity and bold.

Teaching old Norse languages at the University of Michigan is not a normal route into the wine industry but for Clay Thompson and Fredericka Churchill it led straight to the Edna Valley and the establishment of **Claiborne & Churchill** winery in 1983. In 1995 they constructed the first straw bale building in California and the 16-inch thick rice-straw walls ensure that the winery maintains a constant cellar temperature without any heating or air conditioning.

The Santa Cruz Mountains are dotted with small pockets of vineyards hidden by the forested slopes

It has taken over ten years for other wineries to jump onto the environmental bandwagon.

In only 20 years **Talley Vineyards** has become the most recognized name for quality Chardonnay and

Pinot Noir in San Luis Obispo County. The Talleys started out as farmers but saw the potential in Arroyo Grande for grape growing. Their Chardonnay and Pinot Noir are consistently outstanding.

One of America's largest Pinot Noir vineyards sits by the side of Highway 101, three miles south of the town of Arroyo Grande. **Laetitia Vineyard and Winery** started life as Maison Duetz, which concentrated on sparkling wine. When Maison Duetz sold, the new owners minimized sparkling wine production and put their efforts into Pinot Noir and Chardonnay. The results have been progressively good with very well made wines at a realistic price point.

WINERIES & MORE

**Baileyana Winery
Tasting Room**
5828 Orcutt Road
San Luis Obispo, CA 93401
Tel: 805 269 8200
www.baileyana.com
Open daily 10AM–5PM.

Chamisal Vineyards
7525 Orcutt Road
San Luis Obispo,
CA 93401
Tel: 866 808 9463
www.chamisalvineyards.com
Open daily 10AM–5PM.

Saucelito Canyon Winery
3080 Biddle Ranch Road
San Luis Obispo,
CA 93403
Tel: 805 543 2111
www.saucelitocanyon.com
Open daily 10AM–5PM
except major holidays.

**Claiborne &
Churchill Vintners**
2649 Carpenter
Canyon Road
San Luis Obispo, CA 93401
Tel: 805 544 4066
www.claibornechurchill.com
Open daily 11AM–5PM
except major holidays.

Talley Vineyards
3031 Lopez Drive
Arroyo Grande, CA 93420
Tel: 805 489 0446
www.talleyvineyards.com
Open daily
10:30AM–4:30PM.

**Laetitia Vineyard
and Winery**
453 Laetitia Vineyard Drive
Arroyo Grande, CA 93420
Tel: 805 474 7651
www.laetitiawine.com
Open daily 11AM–5PM.
Closed Christmas Day.

WHERE TO STAY AND EAT

San Luis Obispo

ACCOMODATIONS

Apple Farm Inn
2015 Monterey Street
San Luis Obispo, CA 93401
Tel: 805 544 2040
www.applefarm.com

La Cuesta Inn
2074 Monterey Street
San Luis Obispo, CA 93401
Tel: 800 543 2777
www.lacuestainn.com

Madonna Inn
100 Madonna Road
San Luis Obispo, CA 93405
Tel: 805 784 2410
www.madonnainn.com

Shell Beach Inn
653 Shell Beach Road
Shell Beach, CA 93449
Tel: 805 773 4373
www.shellbeachinn.com

RESTAURANTS

Ciopinot
1051 Nipomo Street
San Luis Obispo, CA 93401
Tel: 805 547 1111
www.ciopinotrestaurant.com
Seafood

Novo
726 Higuera Street
San Luis Obispo, CA 93401
Tel: 805 543 3986
www.novorestaurant.com
International cuisine

JIM CLENDENEN OF AU BON CLIMAT

Monterey

de Anza Inn
211 North Freemont Street
Monterey, CA 93940
Tel: 831 646 8300
www.deanzainn.com

The Clement Monterey
750 Cannery Row
Monterey, CA 93940
Tel: 877 859 5095
www.ichotelsgroup.com

Inn at Spanish Bay
2700 17-mile Drive
Pebble Beach, CA 93953
Tel: 800 654 9300
www.pebblebeach.com/
accommodations/the-inn-at-
spanish-bay

RESTAURANT
The Sardine Factory
701 Wave Street
Monterey, CA 9390
Tel: 831 373 3775
www.sardinefactory.com
Seafood

Santa Cruz

ACCOMODATIONS
Dream Inn
175 W. Cliff Drive
Santa Cruz, CA 95060
Tel: 831 426 4330
www.dreaminnsantacruz.com

RESTAURANT
Ristorante Avanti
1711 Mission Street
Santa Cruz, CA 95060
Tel: 831 427 0135
www.ristoranteavanti.com
Italian cuisine

Los Gatos

ACCOMODATIONS
Hotel Los Gatos
210 East Main Street
Los Gatos, CA 95030
Tel: 408 335 1700
www.jdvhotels.com/hotels/
siliconvalley/los_gatos

Toll House
140 South Santa Cruz
Avenue
Los Gatos, CA 95030
Tel: 408 395 7070
www.larkspurhotels.com/
collection/toll-house

RESTAURANT
Manresa
320 Village Lane
Los Gatos, CA 95030
Tel: 408 354 4330
www.manresarestaurant.com
French/Modern Catalan
cuisine

SANTA BARBARA COUNTY

S ANTA BARBARA is the quintessential playground of the rich and famous. The climate is Mediterranean and Spanish-style villas cascade down the mountains to a sweeping bay. It's close enough to Los Angeles, just two hours' drive to the south, to be attractive to the Hollywood crowd and it's to Hollywood that it owes its current status as a wine mecca. The movie *Sideways* put Santa Barbara, more specifically Santa Ynez Valley, on every Pinot Noir lover's map, although great Pinots were being made here long before the movie.

Santa Maria Valley

In the north of the county, just to the south of Arroyo Grande, the Santa Maria Valley stretches inland from Santa Maria town, straddling Highway 101. Take the East Betteravia Road exit through a flat and uninteresting agricultural landscape that gently rises until it gets to the eastern end of the valley, where both the view and the climate change. The 7,500 acres of the Santa Maria Valley AVA are predominantly planted with Chardonnay and Pinot Noir, which are perfectly suited to the cool climate created by fog and coastal breezes penetrating the east-west orientation of the valley. The **Bien Nacido** vineyard in particular has become synonymous with great Pinots and Chardonnays. Wines made from Bien Nacido fruit are all vineyard designate, for which wineries pay a high premium.

Although there are over 30 wineries in the appellation, only a handful have tasting rooms and they are mainly at the eastern end of the valley. The drive from Santa Maria crosses a flat, featureless landscape toward a mountain range.

《 The vineyards of Clos Pepe produce some of the most sought-after Pinot Noir in California

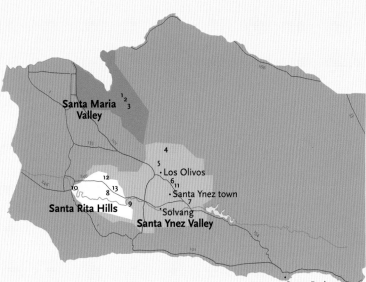

1. Cambria Winery and Vineyard
2. Kenneth Volk Vineyards
3. Foxen Winery and Vineyard
4. Fess Parker Winery and Vineyards
5. Firestone Vineyard
6. Carhartt Vineyard
7. Gainey Vineyard
8. Sanford Winery and Vineyard
9. Alma Rosa Winery
10. Fiddlestix Tasting Room & Winery
11. Longoria Wines
12. Melville Vineyards and Winery
13. Foley Estates

WINE LABELS TO LOOK FOR IN SANTA BARBARA COUNTY

Alma Rosa is the new winery of Richard Sanford, one of the pioneers in the Santa Rita Hills

Just below these mountains is the Santa Maria Bench, a mesa sitting above the Sisquoc River that during the summer months transforms into a dry riverbed. There are vineyards as far as the eye can see. They seem to go on forever and they belong to **Cambria Winery and Vineyard**, part of the Kendall Jackson empire. This is the biggest winery in the valley and although Cambria wines are widely available at very reasonable prices, several very good small-lot wines are made that are only available at the tasting room.

Santa Maria Mesa Road continues past Cambria to Tepusquet Road where the valley narrows. Turning left leads to the former Byron Winery that is now the home of **Kenneth Volk Vineyards**. The original Byron Winery was sold to Robert Mondavi, acquired by Constellation Brands as part of the Mondavi empire, sold off to a farming family who defaulted on their loan and was eventually bought by the Jackson family, owners of Cambria. Such is the convoluted story of many of California's wineries today. Before buying the original Byron Winery, Ken Volk established Wild Horse Winery and Vineyards in Paso Robles that was eventually sold to Constellation Brands. It's a small world! Volk's Chardonnays and Pinots are well-made wines worth the journey to this outpost of Santa Barbara County.

Returning from Kenneth Volk Winery, Tepusquet Road crosses the Sisquoc River and becomes Foxon Canyon Road. The landscape changes from desolate open panoramas to pastoral scenes dotted with oak trees and horse ranches. There is a noticeable increase in temperature, too. Where Santa Ynez Valley starts and Santa Maria Valley ends is hard to tell except that the last Santa Maria tasting room is the rustic **Foxen Winery**, to be found on the left, driving south. This was one of the tasting rooms featured in *Sideways* and is always a popular tourist attraction. The wines here are very small production, vineyard designated wines using a minimalist approach to winemaking. The rustic barn that serves as a tasting room belies the quality of the wines, which frequently score very high points.

Sea Smoke is one of the great cult Pinot Noirs made in Lompoc. The winery is named for the cool maritime fog that slows the ripening of the grapes

Santa Ynez Valley

Santa Ynez Valley is a bucolic paradise after the austere Santa Maria Valley. The vista of rolling hills, ranches, oaks and cattle is almost too picture perfect. This is a finely manicured landscape with nothing out of place. The climate is also different with significantly higher temperatures resulting from lack of marine influence. Cabernet and Merlot grow well here as well as Syrah and Viognier.

Fess Parker Winery and Vineyards is a dramatic contrast to Foxen a few miles down the road. The landscaped grounds suggest an upscale resort and the tasting room is housed in a large, elegant, veranda-surrounded building that could almost be a southern plantation mansion. Fess Parker, who passed away in 2010 at the age of 85, made his name as Davy Crockett in the 1950s movie and television series and started his wine business in 1989. His celebrity guarantees a steady flow of visitors and the tasting room's starring role in *Sideways* doesn't hurt.

The flagship winery of Santa Ynez has always been **Firestone Vineyard** but as impressive as their facility may be, the quality of their wines has not held up. Hopefully this is all about to change. In line with modern Californian wine industry practices the former family business has been purchased by Bill Foley, owner of Foley Vineyards in the Santa Rita Hills. Foley is a financier turned vintner and he has earned considerable respect for his dedication to quality. Firestone is a winery to watch.

Los Olivos

In the center of the Santa Barbara wine country is a cluster of small towns within a few miles of each other. Coming out of Foxen Canyon Road, at the head of Santa Ynez Valley, sits Los Olivos, a one-street Victorian town that has become the wine-tasting capital. Only a few years ago this was a charming, sleepy little town with a couple of tasting rooms, a general store and a 100-year-old stagecoach stop and restaurant, **Mattei's Tavern**. Now, Grand Avenue, the main street through town, has more tasting rooms than any other business. This once quiet little town of 1,000 residents has succumbed to the *Sideways* Effect. Wine rules here. Fess Parker has built an upscale resort and spa in the center of town. Directly across the street **Los Olivos Café** and Wine Merchant, featured in *Sideways* of course, usually has lines of people out of the door; art galleries occupy the few spaces not taken by tasting rooms. The town still holds onto its Victorian charm but has lost its soul.

Richard Longoria opened a tasting room here long before it was fashionable and his wines, which are made at his winery in Lompoc, are among the best in the region. Across Grand Avenue is a tiny, hole-in-the-wall tasting room that shouldn't be overlooked. **Carhartt Vineyard** produces impressive Merlot and Syrah from a ten-acre site planted on a mesa in the heart of Santa Ynez Valley AVA. Their tasting room is promoted as "The World's Smallest" and they could be right.

The funky old tasting room of Foxen Vineyards, featured in the film *Sideways*, belies the quality of the wines

Santa Ynez Town

Leave Los Olivos on Highway 154 and drive past rolling hills and horse ranches to Highway 246. Turn right and enter the town of Santa Ynez. To get to the town proper turn right off Highway 246 but before that, on the left, **Gainey Vineyard** has an elegant tasting room set back from the road and in the summer the landscaped grounds next to the vineyards make an ideal picnic stop. Incongruously, a little further on the same side of the road the **Chumash Casino Resort and Spa** offers a completely un-wine-related experience. It is the actual town of Santa Ynez that's of the most interest and commercialism has mercifully passed it by. There are a couple of small tasting rooms here,

Vineyards line Santa Rosa Road through the Santa Rita Hills

but the real attraction is the ambience of a classic western town complete with false-front buildings and boardwalks. Certainly a visit to the far end of **Sagunto Street** on most evenings is like stepping back into the old Wild West. The historic **Maverick Saloon** attracts top Country and Western bands most nights during the summer, and people are spilling out onto the board-

walk. Next door, **Trattoria Grappolo** is another lively place to spend time over good Italian cuisine.

Solvang

Solvang is undoubtedly the best-known destination in Santa Ynez Valley although it has nothing to do with wine. Danish flags fly from faux windmills alongside half-timbered

restaurants with names like The Red Viking and Little Mermaid and an endless selection of pastry shops. This is Denmark by way of Las Vegas and Disneyland. To be fair, the community was established 100 years ago by a group of Danish educators and has strong Danish and German roots. Today, however, it is one big tourist attraction. Only about 10 percent of the population is of Danish ancestry and they're outnumbered by those of English, Irish and German stock, but this doesn't stop the Danish theme overwhelming the town.

There are a handful of tasting rooms hoping to pick up business from the hordes of tourists that visit every year and one in particular is worth a visit. Jim Clendenen is one of the great characters and winemakers of California. After making outstanding wines under the label Au Bon Climat for 25 years, he has just opened a tasting room in Santa Barbara.

Santa Rita Hills

Drive through Solvang into Buellton, past **The Hitching Post** restaurant with its permanently packed car park—yes, it was featured in *Sideways*—and turn left onto Avenue of the Flags. Follow the road on to Santa Rosa Road in the Santa Rita Hills AVA. The road passes through some of the best Pinot Noir and Chardonnay vineyards in California. Like the Santa Maria Valley, this valley also has an east-west orientation, allowing the marine influence to control the potentially hot climate. As in the other coastal regions this is prime Chardonnay and Pinot Noir terroir.

The first extensive plantings on the south side of the road are the legendary **Sanford and Benedict Vineyard**. A small road leads to the charming tasting room of **Alma Rosa Winery** hidden behind trees.

Richard Sanford is one of the great pioneers of the Santa Barbara wine industry, having planted the first Pinot Noir in the Santa Rita Hills in 1970. After selling his eponymous winery to Terlato Family Wines, he started a new venture with Alma Rosa. Sustainable farming in 100 percent organic vineyards has always been Sanford's passion and the elegant

Pinot Noir and Chardonnay he makes is a testament to the quality of the fruit.

The original **Sanford Winery** is a few miles down the road in a large, environmentally sound, "green" construction, adobe block building surrounded by the La Riconada vineyard. When a large conglomerate takes over a carefully-run family business it frequently does so at the expense of quality. Fortunately this has not happened with Sanford. The wines are a good as ever.

Santa Rosa Road continues past notable vineyards like **Fiddlestix** and **Sea Smoke** high in the Santa Rita range. It eventually reaches Lompoc where many great wines are made by Longoria, Sea Smoke and Loring among others in an industrial warehouse complex on the outskirts of town. None have tasting rooms here. This is major center for the flower seed industry and in early summer the fields around Lompoc are a riot of color.

Leave Lompoc on Highway 246 back toward Buellton for about nine miles. **Melville Winery** on the north side of the road resembles a Mediterranean villa surrounded by estate vineyards and they pour excellent Pinot Noir, Chardonnay and Syrah to savor in their tasting room overlooking a picturesque garden and courtyard. A little further along, **Foley Estates Winery** produces some of the best wines in the appellation and sits surrounded by one of Santa Barbara's largest estate vineyards. This was the first winery of Bill Foley who is rapidly becoming one of California wine industry's major players. He now owns major properties throughout the state including Sebastiani Vineyards in Sonoma, Chalk Hill Winery and a major share in Napa Valley's Kuleto Winery.

WINERIES & MORE

Cambria Winery and Vineyard
5475 Chardonnay Lane
Santa Maria, CA 93454
Tel: 805 938 7318
www.cambriawine.com
Open daily 10AM–5PM.

Kenneth Volk Vineyards
5230 Tepusquet Road
Santa Maria, CA 93454
Tel: 805 938 7896
www.volkwines.com
Open 10:30AM–4:30PM.

**Foxen Winery
and Vineyard**
7200 Foxen Canyon Road
Santa Maria, CA 93454
Tel: 805 937 4251
www.foxenvineyard.com
Open daily 10:30AM–4PM.

**Fess Parker Winery
and Vineyards**
6200 Foxen Canyon Road
Los Olivos, CA 93441
Tel: 805 688 1545
www.fessparker.com
Open daily 10AM–5PM.

Firestone Vineyard
5000 Zaca Station Road
Los Olivos, CA 93441
Tel: 805 688 3940
www.firestonewine.com
Open daily 10AM–5PM.

Carhartt Vineyard
2990A Grand Avenue
Los Olivos, CA 93441
Tel: 805 688 0685
www.carharttvineyard.com
Open 10AM–5PM.
Closed Tues.

Gainey Vineyard
3950 East Highway 246
Santa Ynez, CA 93460
Tel: 805 688 0558
www.gaineyvineyard.com
Open daily 10AM–5PM.

**Au Bon Climat
Tasting Room**
813 Anacapa Street

Santa Barbara, CA 93103
Tel: 805 845 8435
www.aubonclimat.com
Open daily 12AM–6PM.

**Sanford Winery
and Vineyard**
5010 Santa Rosa Road
Lompoc, CA 93436
Tel: 805 375 5900
www.sanfordwinery.com
Open daily except
major holidays.
Sun-Thurs 11AM–4PM,
Fri-Sat 11AM–5PM.

Alma Rosa Winery
7250 Santa Rosa Road
Buellton, CA 93427
Tel: 805 688 9090
www.almarosawinery.com
Open daily 11AM–4:30PM.

**Fiddlestix Tasting Room
& Winery**
1597 East Chestnut Avenue
Lompoc, CA 93436
Tel: 805 742 0204
www.fiddleheadcellars.com
Open Sat 11AM–4PM. Other
days by appointment.

Longoria Wines
2935 Grand Avenue
Los Olivos, CA 93441
Tel: 805 688 0305
www.longoriawine.com
Open daily 11AM–4:30PM.

**Melville Vineyards
and Winery**

STILL WATERS

5185 East Highway 246
Lompoc, CA 93436
Tel: 805 735 7030
www.melvillewinery.com
Open daily 11AM–4PM.

Foley Estates
6121 East Highway 246
Lompoc, CA 93436
Tel: 805 737 6222
www.foleywines.com
Open daily 11AM–5PM.

WHERE TO STAY AND EAT

Buellton

ACCOMODATIONS

A-RU
225 McMurray Road, Ste D
Buellton, CA 93427
Tel: 805 686 9001
Japanese cuisine

The Hitching Post II
406 East Highway 246
Buellton, CA 93427
Tel: 805 688 0676
www.hitchingpost2.com
Steak house

RESTAURANT

Pea Soup Andersen's Inn
51 East Highway 246
Buellton, CA 93472
Tel: 805 688 3216
www.peasoupandersens.com

Los Olivos

ACCOMODATIONS

**Fess Parker's Wine
Country Inn and Spa**
2860 Grand Avenue
Los Olivos, CA 93441
Tel: 805 688 7788
www.fessparker.com

RESTAURANTS

**Brothers Restaurant at
Mattei's Tavern**
2350 Railway Avenue

SANFORD WINERY

Los Olivos, CA 93441
Tel: 805 688 4820
www.matteistavern.com

Los Olivos Café
2879 Grand Avenue
Los Olivos, CA 93441
Tel: 805 688 7265
www.losolivoscafe.com

Solvang

ACCOMODATIONS
Hadsten House
1450 Mission Drive
Solvang, CA 93436
Tel: 805 688 3210
www.hadstenhouse.com

**Wine Valley Inn
and Cottages**
1564 Copenhagen Drive
Solvang, CA 93463
Tel: 800 824 6444
www.winevalleyinn.com

RESTAURANTS
Mirabelle
409 First Street
Solvang, CA 93463
Tel: 805 688 1703
www.solvanginns.com/mi-rabelle_restaurant.html

**Mortensen's
Danish Bakery**
1588 Mission Drive
Solvang, CA 93463
Tel: 805 688 8373

SOUTERN CALIFORNIA

IT'S NO COINCIDENCE that most serious books on California wine omit Southern California. Quite honestly, unless you are already in the area it may not be worth the detour. This just isn't the best place to grow quality grapes but it doesn't stop people from trying.

Temecula

The only concentration of wineries in Southern California is in the Temecula Valley in Riverside County. Apparently the name Temecula is derived from a Native American term for "land where sun shines through the mist," which would suggest vineyards should thrive here. Then again this may have been concocted by a savvy PR company. Most of the land is close to 1,200 feet high and cool Pacific air is drawn into the valley through two gaps in the coastal mountains by the heat rising from the inland desert. None of this seemed to help the quality of the wines, however. In the 1990s the vineyards were decimated by Pierce's Disease, spread by the glassy-winged sharpshooter, and the area under vine declined from 2,300 to 1,300 acres. To make matters worse, Allied Domecq, which owned Callaway Winery, sold off 300 acres for residential development. Callaway is now in single-family ownership.

The good news is that replanting has replaced Chardonnay with pest-resistant red varietals from the Rhône, Italy and Spain that are far more suited to this terroir and hopefully will raise the quality of the wines.

Temecula may not be worth a major detour for the serious oenophile, but for anyone driving from Los Angeles to Palm Springs it's certainly worth stopping by. Most wineries

« A signpost points the way to the boutique wineries along Temecula's De Portola Wine Trail

1. Bella Vista Cilurzo Vineyard and Winery
2. Callaway Vineyard and Winery
3. Bernardo Winery
4. Hacienda de las Rosas Tasting Room
5. San Pasqual Winery
6. San Antonio Winery
7. Cornell Winery & Tasting Room
8. Rosenthal—the Malibu Estate

WINE LABELS TO LOOK FOR IN SOUTHERN CALIFORNIA

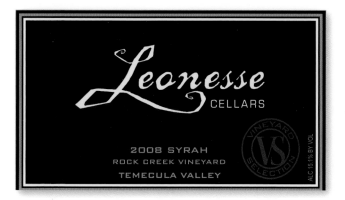

Cougar Vineyards tasting room pours some of the most interesting wines in Temecula

are very visitor friendly, often with picnic facilities. Vincenzo Cilurzo, who retired in 2004, planted the first commercial vineyard in 1968. The new owners renamed the winery **Bella Vista Vineyard and Winery** and are having some success with Petite Syrah.

South Coast Winery, Resort and Spa is the biggest operation in Temecula, with deluxe villas and an award-winning restaurant. The tasting room and restaurant have sweeping vineyard views. Opened in 2003, this is more Napa in character than Temecula.

The greatest concentration of wineries is along Rancho California Road

but some of the most interesting wineries line De Portola Road and include **Cougar Vineyards** and **Robert Renzoni Winery**. They specialize in Mediterranean varieties that appear to thrive here although a significant amount of fruit is shipped in from other areas such as Paso Robles.

Ballooning is a popular activity here and every June the **Temecula Valley Balloon and Wine Festival** combines the best of both worlds, although it's perhaps wise to find a pilot who doesn't drink! Old Town Temecula has become a popular center for antique hunting and the false-front buildings have a certain charm that reflects the atmosphere of the Old West.

San Diego County

The first wine grapes planted in California were at the Misíon San Diego de Alcalá in 1781. The wines made here tend to stay here and there is virtually no market outside the county so if you want the novelty of tasting San Diego County wines you have to go there.

Bernardo Winery has been here since 1889 and is the oldest continually operating winery in San Diego County but judging from the wines, experience and longevity don't relate to quality. How do they stay in business? Perhaps the 13 artist village shops on the winery estate help, along with Café Merlot and the Sweet Pea Coffee Shop, while every Friday morning there's a farmers' market. The winery has been made into a family destination and even if this isn't an enophile's dream it provides a pleasant distraction for a couple of hours if you happen to be nearby.

In Old Town San Diego, the heart of the city's tourism area, Hacienda de las Rosas Tasting Room makes up for its wines with costumed tasting room staff and an 1800s atmosphere. The wines are made at the winery in nearby Ramona from locally grown fruit.

Also in San Diego is San Pasqual Winery, which sources fruit from local San Diego County wineries and also from the Guadalupe Valley in nearby Baja California, Mexico.

Los Angeles

One of the world's biggest cities may seem like the most unlikely place to make wine but at one time there were over 100 wineries in Los Angeles River Basin. Now only one remains and it's located right in the heart of downtown L.A. San Antonio Winery has been making wine here since 1917 and weathered Prohibition by producing sacramental wines for the churches and parishes of Los Angeles County. By the repeal of Prohibition in 1933 it was one of the few wineries left in Southern California. The winery still occupies its original building that has been designated as a Los Angeles Cultural Monument.

This may sound like a novelty winery but don't be deceived. The wines are in general well worth tasting. The Riboli family who own the winery have purchased vineyards in prime areas such as the Santa Lucia Highlands and Napa's Rutherford AVA and have long-term relationships with growers throughout Northern California. They own winemaking facilities east of Paso Robles and this is where they make red wines, but whites are still made in downtown Los Angeles. The fruit is crushed in Paso and then taken to Los Angles for vinification.

The exclusive Los Angeles suburb of Bel Air is better known for the homes of movie stars than winemakers but up in the hills above the multimillion-dollar mansions Tom and Ruth Jones planted vineyards in 1978 and established **Moraga Winery**. Just two wines are made from the 9.5-acre vineyard, a Bordeaux-style red and Sauvignon Blanc.

Both wines are very well made. Unfortunately there is no tasting room or public access.

Malibu

Think of sun, sand and surf and then think again. The mountains above Malibu offer a terroir high above the coastal fog and perfect for growing grapes. There are now over 50 vineyards and wineries hidden in the Santa Monica Mountains but most of them are closed to the public.

There is one notable exception. In 1987, LA businessman George Rosenthal planted vines at 1,400 feet on his 250-acre Malibu estate after two years of research. The estate is only open for special events but **Rosenthal** wines can be sampled at their tasting room right on the Pacific Coast Highway.

Production at all the Malibu wineries is tiny and most of the wines never leave the neighborhood. The good news is that many of the wines made here can be tasted at **Cornell Winery**

Leonesse Cellars offers an eclectic mix of wineriese ≫

and Tasting Room up on Mulholland Drive and this may well be the only chance you will ever have to taste them.

WINERIES & MORE

Bella Vista Vineyard and Winery
41220 Calle Contento
Temecula, CA 92592
Tel: 951 676 5250
www.bellavistawinery.com
Open daily 10AM–6PM.

Callaway Vineyard and Winery
32720 Rancho California Road
Temecula, CA 92592
Tel: 951 676 4001
www.callawaywinery.com
Open daily 10AM–5PM.

Cougar Vineyard and Winery
39870 De Portola Road
Temecula, CA 92592
Tel: 951 491 0825
www.cougervineyards.com
Open daily 11AM–6PM.

Robert Renzoni Winery
37350 De Portola Road
Temecula, CA 92592
Tel: 951 302 8466
www.robertrenzonivineyards.com
Open daily 11AM–6PM.

Bernardo Winery
13330 Paseo Del Verano Norte
San Diego, CA 92128
Tel: 858 487 1866

RENZZONI WINERY, TEMECULA

www.bernardowinery.com
Open daily 10AM–5PM.

**Hacienda de las Rosas
Tasting Room**
Plaza del Pasado—
Juan Street Entrance
2764 Calhoun Street
San Diego, CA 92110
Tel: 619 840 5579
www.haciendawinery.com
Sun-Thurs 11:30AM–7PM,
Fri-Sat 11:30AM–9PM.

San Pasqual Winery
5151 Santa Fe Street, Ste H
San Diego, CA 92109
Tel: 858 270 7550
www.sanpasqualwinery.com
Open Sat 12PM-4PM.

San Antonio Winery
Plaza San Antonio
737 Lamar Street

Los Angeles, CA 90031
Tel: 323 223 1401
www.sanantoniowinery.com
Open daily 9AM–7PM.

**Cornell Winery
& Tasting Room**
29975 Mulholland
Highway
Cornell, CA 91301
Tel: 818 735 3542
www.cornellwinery.com
Open Thurs-Sun
10AM–6PM.

**Rosenthal—
the Malibu Estate**
26023 Pacific Coast
Highway,
Malibu, CA 90265
Tel: 310 456 1392
www.rosenthalestatewines
Open Wed-Thu 1PM-6PM,
Fri-Sun 11AM–6PM.

WHERE TO STAY AND EAT

Temecula

ACCOMODATIONS

Hampton Inn and Suites
28109 Jefferson Avenue
Temecula, CA 92590
Tel: 951 506 2331
www.hamptoninn.hilton.com

Public House
41971 Main Street
Temecula, CA 92590
Tel: 951 676 7305
www.publichouse.tv

San Diego County

ACCOMODATIONS

La Costa Resort and Spa
2100 Costa del Mar Road
Carlsbad, CA 92009

Tel: 800 854 5000
www.lacosta.com

RESTAURANT

West Steak Seafood Spirits
4980 Avenida Encinas
Carlsbad, CA 92008
Tel: 760 930 9100
www.weststeakkandseafood.com
Steak house

Los Angeles

ACCOMODATIONS

Millennium Biltmore Hotel
506 South Grand Avenue
Los Angeles, CA 90071
Tel: 213 624 1011
www.millenimhotels.com

Omni Los Angeles
at California Plaza
251 South Olive Street
Los Angeles. CA 90012
Tel: 213 617 3300
www.omnihotels.com

RESTAURANT

Water Grill
544 South Grand
Los Angeles, CA 90071
Tel: 213 891 0900
www.watergrill.com
Seafood

Malibu

ACCOMODATIONS

Casa Malibu Inn
on the Beach
22752 Pacific Coast
Highway
Malibu, CA 90265
Tel: 310 456 2219

RESTAURANTS

Nobu Malibu
3838 Cross Creek Road
Site 18A
Malibu, CA 90265
Tel: 310 317 9140
www.nobumatsuhisa.com
Japanese cuisine

Sage Room
28915 Pacific Coast
Highway
Malibu, CA 90265
Tel: 310 457 0711
www.malibusageroom.com
Italian cuisine

**Temecula wineries offer an easy
escape from frenetic Los Angeles**

CENTRAL VALLEY

C ALIFORNIA'S GREAT CENTRAL VALLEY is one
the major agricultural areas of the world. Although
Napa Valley is synonymous with California wine,
most of the state's wine production is from this long,
hot swathe of rich agricultural land that stretches from
Redding, north of Sacramento, 400 miles south to Bakers-
field. Neither the soil nor the climate lend themselves to
quality wine grape production but this has not stopped
the industry giants, notably the E & J Gallo Winery
in Modesto, from mass-producing wine. E & J Gallo is
the world's largest family-owned winery and the biggest
exporter of California wine, which has not necessarily
been good for California wine's reputation. To many,
Gallo is synonymous with Thunderbird and Night Train
Express, two fortified wines usually hidden by brown
bags on tenderloin street corners. Gallo also produces the
best-selling sparkling wine in America. André Champagne
(the Champagne designation was grandfathered in) has
been described as "much like ginger ale—pale yellow in
color, lemony and on the sweet side, with maybe an apple
flavor as well and low bubbles." This is being generous but
at around US$5 a bottle it obviously finds an appreciative
market. In spite of its name, it is not made by the *méthode
champenoise* but by bulk fermentation. It shows.

Gallo owns so many labels it can be confusing but if the
address is listed on the label as Modesto, the chances are
it's a Gallo wine.

To be fair, the quality of many of the Gallo wines has
improved over the past decade and some of their brands are
not bad. It has purchased both Louis Martini and William
Hill wineries in Napa Valley and is bringing both wineries
back to their former glory. Gallo of Sonoma, which is an
entirely separate operation run by the grandchildren of

<< Vineyards are overtaking traditional agriculture around Lodi in
   California's Central Valley

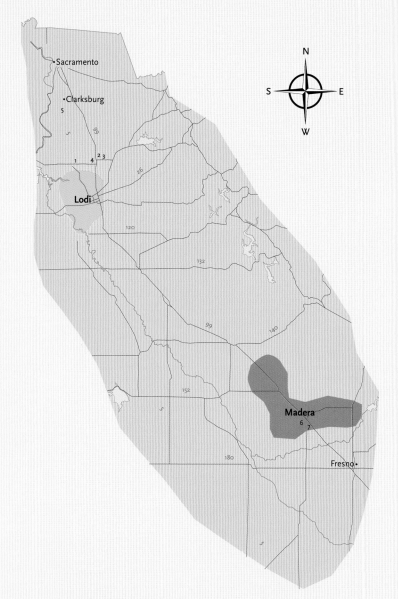

1. Michael-David Winery and Phillips Farm Fruitstand Café
2. Woodbridge by Robert Mondavi
3. Berghold Vineyards & Winery
4. Grands Amis Winery
5. Bogle Winery
6. Quady Winery
7. Ficklin Vineyards

WINE LABELS TO LOOK
FOR IN CENTRAL VALLEY

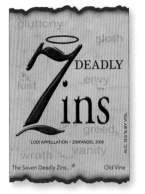

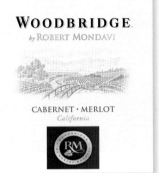

Andrew Quady makes exceptional dessert wines at his eponymous
winery in Madera

Orange Muscat is made into Essencia at Quady Winery in Madera

E & J Gallo, is producing wines of excellent quality.

These mega wineries of the Central Valley generally don't allow visitors, maybe because their industrial scale detracts from the image of hand-crafted, artisanal production. However there are two corners of the valley that are actively promoting wine tourism and making wines that are respectable if not great.

Lodi

On the edge of the Sacramento River Delta, a few miles south of Sacramento, the state capital, Lodi has long been a major center for grape growing. The cooling effect of the delta causes the frequently blistering summer temperatures to plummet at night, creating the ideal environment for many of the more robust varieties of grape. Zinfandel has traditionally been one of the most successful grapes grown here and the fruit is used by wineries in both Napa and Sonoma.

Lodi is a typical small Central Valley agricultural town surrounded by a flat agricultural landscape. Perhaps the town's greatest claim to fame is as the birthplace of A & W Root Beer and A & W Restaurants, established in 1919 and considered to be the original fast food restaurants. Lodi is a sleepy little town with little of interest for the visitor other than a series of food and wine related events throughout the year, developed to attract tourism. The Lodi Grape Festival, Taste of Lodi and Zinfest are the most notable of these.

In recent years, grape farmers have been seduced by the profits that can be made from making the wine themselves and a flourishing wine industry has developed, helped in no small way by the construction of Robert Mondavi's Woodbridge facility. One of the most successful of these is the **Michael-David Winery**. Six generations of the Phillips family have farmed in Lodi and it's the fifth generation brothers, Michael and David Phillips, who put the family on the wine map with their highly successful 7 Deadly Zins, a blend from seven vineyards in Lodi. You can find better Zinfandels in California, but you would be hard pressed to find one marketed as successfully. A typical roadside fruit stand originally devoted to the fruit and vegetables of

Phillips Farms fronts the winery. The fruit stand has grown to include a café, bakery and tasting room and the down-home atmosphere belies the scale of the winery to the rear.

Woodbridge by Robert Mondavi, now owned by Constellation Brands, gives one of the few opportunities in California to experience wine production on a large scale. Constellation Brands, the largest wine company in the world, acquired the winery after a particularly acrimonious Mondavi family feud. The Mondavi name is still invoked, however, to sell the wines. Their Woodbridge plant offers tours by appointment.

Many of the wineries have tasting rooms and the **Lodi Wine and Visitor Center** is a good starting point. Interactive exhibits and a Wines of Lodi tasting bar give an overview of the area, but more importantly they have wine trail maps available to guide you on your way through the vineyards. Most of the establishments are very modest by Napa and Sonoma standards but an exception is **Berghold Estate Winery**. The tasting room, set in landscaped gardens with marble fountains and 1,500 rose bushes, could be transplanted to Napa without looking out of place. Owners Joe and Kay Berghold have been long-time collectors and the interior of the tasting room houses one of the largest collections of American Victorian antiques in the country. The majority of Berghold wines are red varieties and very reasonably priced.

Many Lodi wineries only sell their wines at the winery and prices tend to be high for the quality of wine being made. For the best overview of the area with one-stop shopping, just to the east of Lodi in Lockeford, the **Vino Piazza** is a collection of 75 boutique wineries and tasting rooms in one location. Each is independently owned and operated and each has its own tasting schedule. Check the website.

Clarksburg

A few miles north of Lodi, 7,000 acres of vines form the Clarksburg AVA. Sitting in the flat Sacramento River delta, this area is isolated from the rest of California's wine country. Twenty-five varieties of grape are grown here, seemingly with little consideration as to whether or not this is appropriate terroir. Most of the grapes are grown for sale to wineries outside the area, including Sutter Home in Napa. Access is from either Interstate 80 or Interstate 5 and there is really absolutely no reason to be here unless it's to visit **Bogle Winery**, the only significant one within the AVA. Like so many grape growers in this region, the Bogle family has been involved in farming for several generations and they planted their first vines in 1968. They make wines from just about any grape that grows in Clarksburg, and some are even worth drinking!

Madera

Madera, 120 miles southeast of Lodi, is an even more lackluster agricultural town, surrounded by a similarly flat, featureless agricultural landscape. Although you are unlikely to stumble across them by accident, there is a cluster of a dozen wineries to the south of Madera, most of which could not justify being considered a destination in their own right. This

Sixth generation farmers, the Phillips brothers have been master marketers of their Lodi wines

is not an area known for fine wine grapes, but with astronomical land prices in prime wine regions such as Napa and Sonoma, Madera offers an affordable entry into the world of wine. The **Madera Wine Trail** may not merit a special journey, but for the enophile visiting Yosemite or Sequoia National Parks it might be worth a detour.

Madera is the home of Cooks Champagne, another member of the Constellation Brands stable of wineries and another producer of cheap sparkling wine made by secondary fermentation, which can do nothing to improve Franco-American relations. The winery is in a barbed-wire protected, guarded compound that doesn't exactly exude a welcoming atmosphere. But just around the corner is the jewel of the Madera wine industry. Andrew and Laurel **Quady** started their eponymous winery in 1997 and they have sensibly concentrated on making wines that are appropriate

Lodi Wine & Visitor Center gives a complete overview of the area and the opportunity to taste many of the region's wines

for the area. They specialize in dessert wines that are a delight to drink. Essensia is made from the Orange Muscat grape that gives the wine a beautiful floral nose, Elysium is made from the Black Muscat grape and other successes include Starboard, a Californian port, and even vermouth.

America's best-known

port is also made in Madera at **Ficklin Vineyards.** Winery tours can get repetitive, since every winery is fundamentally the same, but port production is different and here you can see the traditional solera blending system. Even better is the free tasting of their different ports at the end of the tour.

WINERIES & MORE

**Michael-David Winery
and Phillips Farm
Fruitstand Café**
4580 West Highway 12
Lodi, CA 95242
Tel: 209 368 7384
www.lodivineyards.com
Open daily 10AM–5PM.

**Woodbridge by
Robert Mondavi**
5950 East Woodbridge Rd
Acampo, CA 95220
Tel: 209 365 8139
www.woodbridgewines.com
Open daily
10:30AM–4:30PM
except major holidays.

**Berghold Vineyards
& Winery**
17343 North Cherry Road
Lodi, CA 95240
Tel: 209 333 9291
www.bergholdvineyards.com
Open Thurs-Sun
11AM–5PM.

Grands Amis Winery
115 North School Street,
Suite 5 (in downtown)
Lodi, CA 95242
Tel: 209 369 6805
www.grandsamis.com
Open Fri-Sun 1PM-5PM.

Bogle Winery
37783 Road 144
Clarksburg, CA 95612
Tel: 916 744 1139
www.boglewinery.com
Open Mon-Fri 10AM–5PM,
Sat-Sun 11AM–5PM
except major holidays.

Quady Winery
13181 Road 24
Madera, CA 93639
Tel: 559 673 8068
www.quadywinery.com
Open Mon-Fri
9:30AM–4:30PM,
Sat-Sun 12PM-4:30PM.

Ficklin Vineyards
30246 Avenue 7
Madera, CA 93637
Tel: 559 661 0075
www.ficklin.com
Open daily 11AM–5PM.

ATTRACTIONS
**Lodi Wine
& Visitor Center**
2545 West Turner Road
Lodi, CA 95242
Tel: 209 365 0621
www.lodiwine.com
Open daily 10AM–5PM.

Vino Piazza
12470 Locke Road
Lockeford, CA 95237
Tel: 800 939 2566
www.vinopiazza.com

WHERE TO STAY AND EAT

Lodi

ACCOMODATIONS

Wine and Roses Hotel, Restaurant & Spa
2505 West Turner Road
Lodi, CA 95240
Tel: 209 334 6988
www.winerose.com

Holiday Inn Express
1337 East Kettleman Lane
Lodi, CA 95240
Tel: 209 210 0150
www.hiexpress.com

RESTAURANT

Alebrijes Mexican Grill
1301 West Lockeford Street
Lodi, CA 95242
Tel: 209 368 1831
www.alebrijesbistro.com

Madera

ACCOMODATIONS

Spring Hill Suites
1219 East Almond Avenue
Madera, CA 93637
Tel: 559 664 9800
www.marriott.com/hotels/
travel/fatmd-springhill-suites-
madera

RESTAURANT

Vineyard
605 South I Street
Madera, CA 93637
Tel: 559 674 0923
www.vineyardrestaurant.com

PHILLIPS FARM FRUITSTAND, LODI

SIERRA FOOTHILLS

Highway 49 meanders from one small, charming Wild West town to the next along the western edge of the Sierra Nevada Mountains. This route was the foundation of modern California, connecting one gold mine to the next during the 1849 Gold Rush from which the highway derives its name.

Three adjacent counties house most of the wineries: El Dorado, Amador and Calaveras. The gold mines are gone and the new gold is wine. The miners introduced vines here soon after 1849 and by the 1870s wineries were well-established, providing libations to the growing work-force. Prohibition put an end to the industry and it wasn't until the 1970s that the price of land in Napa and Sonoma encouraged prospective vintners to look farther afield. A surprisingly large number of vines were still clinging on to existence. Many of them dated back over 100 years and old-vine Zinfandel has become the region's signature wine. The gnarly, head-trained vines line tortuous, winding back roads linking one false-front boardwalk town to the next.

Most of the wineries are very small, producing just a few thousand cases a year, and the quality can vary dramatically. The very nature of the landscape creates a wide range of microclimates that enable everything from Zinfandel to Riesling to be grown with varying degrees of success. Many of the wines produced are big, high-alcohol fruit bombs that buck the trend toward more elegant, high-acid food-friendly wines.

The journey along **Highway 49** is in itself a fascinating trip through Californian history and the wineries should be considered an added bonus. Springtime is especially beautiful when the hillsides are green and temperatures have yet to reach the searing heat of summer.

《 Workers move barrels at Terre Rouge winery in Amador County, which specializes in Rhône-style wines

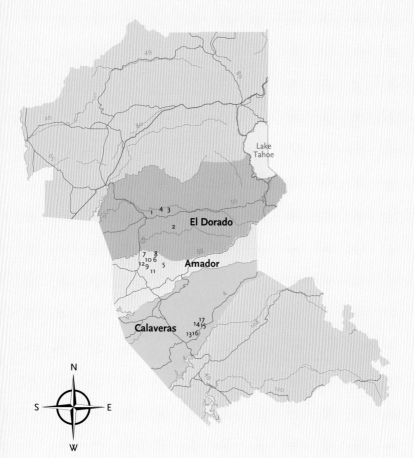

Lake
Tahoe

4 3
1
El Dorado
2

7 8
10 6
12 9 11 5
Amador

Calaveras
17
14 15
13 16

N
S   E
W

1. Boeger Winery
2. Sierra Vista Vine-
   yards & Winery
3. Madroña Vineyards
4. Lava Cap Winery
5. Sobon Estate
6. Shenandoah
   Vineyards
7. Story Winery
8. Renwood Winery

9. Terre Rouge
10. Karly Wines
11. Monteviña Winery
12. Vino Noceto Winery
13. Ironstone Vineyards
14. Stevenot Winery
15. Black Sheep Vintners
16. Chatom Winery
17. Milliaire Winery

WINE LABELS TO LOOK
FOR IN THE
SIERRA FOOTHILLS

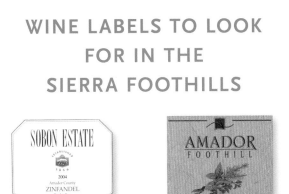

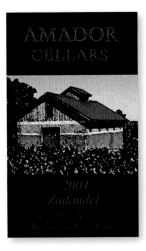

El Dorado County wineries are among the highest in California

El Dorado County

The vineyards of El Dorado County are among the highest in the Foothills, rising up to almost 4,000 feet above sea level. Although there are a handful of wineries in Nevada County to the north, El Dorado is the northernmost county to have a serious concentration of producers, all within a short distance of Placerville, the county seat. Wineries in El Dorado County claim that this terroir helps to produce the region's most elegant wines, including cooler climate varietals such as Riesling and Chardonnay.

The **Boeger** family established their winery on the site of a 19th-century distillery in 1972 and the following year planted vineyards. Pear orchards were planted after Prohibition but disease devastated the whole orchard industry. When the Boegers bought the property there were a few vines left from the 1800s and the fruit is still used in their Zinfandel bottlings. The vineyards are planted on steep hills and Barbera has become a signature wine.

Sierra Vista Vineyards was established in the same year as Boeger in 1972 but it wasn't until 1977 that they had their first crush with fruit purchased from local growers. Studies by John MacCready, the owner, established that the terroir of this area is very similar to that of the northern Rhône, and Sierra Vista has since focused on Rhône varietals—Syrah, Grenache, Mourvèdre, Cinsault, Viognier and Rousanne—with considerable success. This was the first Foothills winery to install solar panels in the 1990s, since when it's been a leader in sustainable practices.

Madroña Vineyards is one of the highest in California with cool nights following hot days. Both Bordeaux and Rhône varietals are grown here and they produce a number of dessert wines including a port and late harvest Zinfandel.

Another old pear orchard was purchased by David and Jeanne Jones, who thought the rich volcanic soil, high elevation, gentle slopes and abundant water would translate into first-class grapes. **Lava Cap Winery**, which opened in 1981, now produces several Rhône-style wines along with Cabernet Sauvignon, Merlot, Chardonnay, Sauvignon Blanc and a surprisingly elegant Zinfandel. A picnic on the winery's deck gives expansive views of the South Fork of the American River. Light picnic fare is available at the winery.

WINERIES & MORE

Boeger Winery
1709 Carson Road
Placerville, CA 95667
Tel: 530 622 8094
www.boegerwinery.com
Open daily 10AM–5PM.

Sierra Vista Vineyards & Winery
4560 Cabernet Way
Placerville, CA 95667
Tel: 530 622 7221
www.sierravistawinery.com
Open daily 10AM–5PM.

Madroña Vineyards
2560 High Hill Road
Camino, CA 95709
Tel: 530 644 5948
www.MadronaVineyards.com
Open daily 10AM–5PM.

Lava Cap Winery
2221 Fruitridge Road
Placerville, CA 95667
Tel: 530 621 0175
www.lavacap.com
Open daily 11AM–5PM.

Amador County

After the lofty vineyards of El Dorado County, adjacent Amador County has the lowest elevations of the Foothills appellations but still sits well over 1,000 feet in altitude. The temperatures are higher here, resulting in big, high-alcohol wines. The heart of the county is the **Shenandoah Valley**, which is actually a high mesa between two rivers. The Shenandoah Valley AVA has the biggest concentration of wineries in the Gold Country and it is arguably the most picturesque, with quaint villages along winding country roads.

Sobon Estate is housed in the old D'Agostini Winery. Founded in 1856, this is one of California's oldest and is now a California State Historic Landmark. Leon and Shirley Sobon bought

Shenandoah Valley in Amador County has the highest concentration of premium wineries in the Sierra foothills

the winery for each other in 1989 for their 30th wedding anniversary. Old-vine Zinfandel was retained and other areas were replanted with Rhône varietals and new Zinfandel vines. This is more than just a winery. It is home to the **Shenandoah Valley Museum** with exhibits on early agriculture and winemaking.

The Sobon's first winery is **Shenandoah Valley Vineyards**, just a few miles from Sobon Estate. It was established in 1977 after Leon left his career as a Senior Scientist with Lockheed Research Lab in Palo Alto, California. They produce only estate-grown wines from organically grown grapes. An art gallery at the winery has revolving exhibits of art and ceramics.

Story Winery is one of the few that still grow Mission grapes introduced by the Spanish missionaries in the 19th Century. They specialize in big, bold Zinfandels that are some of the best of their style, although their power overshadows any possibility of subtlety or complexity. All the fruit is farmed organically. Perhaps the best reason to visit Story is for the view of the Shenandoah Valley from beneath ancient oak trees around the winery's picnic site.

Renwood Winery is one of the largest in the Gold Country, producing over 100,000 cases a year. It was founded in 1993 and became one of the few wineries to achieve a national reputation for its outstanding Zinfandels, in particular the Renwood Grandpère Zinfandel produced from the oldest clone of Zinfandel in America, dating back to the 1860s. In addition to the big, jammy Zins they also make Syrahs and Barberas. Renwood's high profile attracts crowds, and weekends are best avoided.

Terre Rouge produces exclusively Rhône-style wines from fruit sourced throughout the Sierra Foothills. The wines are very well made with good balance and complexity. Winemaker Bill Easton also makes wines such as Cabernet Sauvignon, Zinfandel and Sauvignon Blanc under the Easton Wines label. Both can be tasted at the Terre Rouge tasting room.

Karly was one of the first truly boutique wineries in the region. It was started as a hobby by ex-fighter pilot Buck Cobb and developed into a respected producer of Zinfandel and Mediterranean varietals. This tiny remote winery sits at the end of a half-mile drive through oaks and vineyards complete with wild turkeys.

By far the biggest winery in the region is **Monteviña**. When it was established in 1970 it was a leading player in the Gold Country wine renaissance and quickly became known for big reds such as Zinfandel and Barbera. In 1988 the Trinchero family, of Napa's Sutter Home fame, bought the winery but they have managed to keep the boutique feel of the original property

Monteviña Winery in Amador County specializes in Italian grape varieties

and expanded the range of Italian varietals being produced.

Vino Noceto lies at the other end of the spectrum. The small, family-owned property just produces one wine and does it extremely well. It all started in 1990 with the release of 110 cases of their first vintage of Sangiovese and it has grown to over 9,000 cases a year. Owners Jim and Suzy Gullett decided that Sangiovese was the best warm weather varietal for their vineyard considering that there was a glut of Zinfandel and confusion about Syrah. Their decision certainly paid off.

WINERIES & MORE

Sobon Estate
14430 Shenandoah Road
Plymouth, CA 95669
Tel: 209 245 6554
www.sobonwine.com
Open daily 9:30AM–5PM.

Shenandoah Vineyards
12300 Steiner Road
Plymouth, CA 95669
Tel: 209 245 4455
Open 10AM–5PM.

Story Winery
10525 Bell Road
Plymouth, CA 95669
Tel: 209 245 6208
www.zin.com
Open daily 11AM–5PM.

Renwood Winery

12225 Steiner Road
Plymouth, CA 95669
Tel: 209 245 6979
www.renwood.com
Open daily
10:30AM–5:30PM May-Dec,
Thurs-Sun, Jan-Apr.

Terre Rouge

Dickson Road, just off
Shenandoah Road
Plymouth, CA 95629
Tel: 209 245 3117
www.terrerougewines.com
Open Fri-Mon
11AM–4PM.

Karly Wines

11076 Bell Road
Plymouth, CA 95669
Tel: 209 245 3922
www.karlywines.com
Open daily 12PM-4PM.

Monteviña Winery

20680 Shenandoah
School Road
Plymouth, CA 95669
Tel: 209 245 6942
www.montevina.com
Open daily 10AM–4:30PM.

Vino Noceto Winery

11011 Shenandoah Road
Plymouth, CA 95669
Tel: 209 245 6556
www.noceto.com
Open 11AM–4PM Mon-Fri,
11AM–5PM Sat-Sun.

Calaveras County

Most of the Calaveras
County wineries are clustered near the tiny Gold
Rush town of Murphys.
This one-street settlement
has considerable charm
and the tree-lined single
street is home to several
tasting rooms. Although
the county was a winemaking center during the Gold
Rush, it's only in the past
couple of decades that
there has been a resurgence
with a total of 25 wineries
now in operation. Nearly
all the wineries are small
with limited production
and Zinfandel rules here
as it does in the rest of the
Sierra Foothills.

There is one notable
exception, however. **Ironstone Winery** was established in 1989 and is now
self-described as California's
largest winery entertainment complex. The winery
is almost incidental. There
is a **Heritage Museum** with
the largest crystalline gold
leaf specimen in the world,
weighing in at 44 pounds. A
jewelry shop, culinary center, an Alhamara Theater
Pipe Organ, lakeside park
and amphitheater with
headliner concerts during

Calaveras County Big Trees State Park, just a short drive away, gives a close-up experience of giant sequoias, the world's biggest trees.

Wineries

Ironstone Vineyards
1894 Six Mile Road
Murphys, CA 95247
Tel: 209 728 1251
Open daily 10AM–5PM.

the summer complete the enterprise. Incidentally, there is also a tasting room.

Stevenot Winery, the second biggest in Calaveras although a long way behind Ironstone, has recently changed ownership and a new tasting room is planned for Murphys Main Street. During the 1980s their best seller was white Zinfandel. No more need be said. Many of the tiny boutique wineries offer a peaceful way to pass a summer afternoon but don't expect any earth-shattering tasting experiences. At best the wines will be little more than quaffable but half the fun is finding the unexpected hidden gem.

If you tire of wine tasting, **Moaning Cavern** and **Mercer Cavern** offer guided underground adventures and for the claustrophobic,

Stevenot Winery
458 Main Street #3
Murphys, CA 95217
Tel: 209 728 0148
www.stevenot.com
Open daily 11AM–5PM.

Black Sheep Vintners
221 Main Street
Murphys, CA 95247
Tel: 209 728 2157
www.blacksheepwinery.com
Open daily 11AM–5PM.

Chatom Winery
1969 Highway 4
Douglas Flat, CA 95247
Tel: 209 736 6500
www.chatomvineyards.com
Open daily 11AM–5PM.

Milliaire Winery
276 Main Street
Murphys, CA 95247
Tel: 209 728 1658
www.milliairewinery.com
Open daily 11AM–5PM.

WHERE TO STAY AND EAT

RESTAURANTS

Café Luna
451 Main Street
Placerville, CA 95667
Tel: 530 642 8669

Zachery Jaques Restaurant
1821 Pleasant Valley Rd
Placerville, CA 95667
Tel: 530 626 8045

Twisted Fork
53 Main Street
Sutter Creek, CA 95685
Tel: 209 267-5211

Grounds
402 Main Street
Murphys, CA 95247
Tel: 209 728 8663

Firewood Café
420 Main Street
Murphys, CA
Tel: 209 728 3248

ACCOMODATIONS

GlenMorey
Country House
801 Morey Drive
Placerville, CA 95667
Tel: 209 728 1818
placervillebedandbreakfst.com

The Seasons
2934 Bedford Avenue
Placerville, CA 95667
Tel: 530 626 4420
www.theseasons.net

Plymouth House Inn
9525 Main Street
Plymouth, CA 95669
Tel: 209 245 3298
www.plymouthhouseinn.com

Sutter Creek Inn
75 Main Street
Sutter Creek, CA 95685
Tel: 209 267 5606
www.suttercreekinn.com

Murphys Historic
Hotel & Restaurant
457 Main Street
Murphys, CA 95247
Tel: 209 728 3444
www.murphyshotel.com

Querencia B&B
4383 Sheep Ranch Road
Murphys, CA 95247
Tel: 209 728 9520
www.querencia.ws

Murphys Inn Motel
76 Main Street
Murphys, CA 95247
Tel: 209 728 1818
www.murphysinnmotel.com

Shenandoah Vineyards, founded by Leon Sobon, is one of the earlier vineyards in the Shenandoah appellation »

BEYOND WINE

Brandy

Mention California brandy and the big brands come to mind. Some of the biggest wine producers also distill a significant quantity of brandy. Look on supermarket shelves and the brandies you will see are E & J Gallo, Christian Brothers, Paul Masson and Korbel and these are certainly not the fine Cognacs you hope for at the end of a great meal. They may look like cognac but have a harshness and lack of complexity that make them more suitable for use in the kitchen than for lingering over in a crystal snifter. The warm amber color, which is the result of years of barrel aging in Cognac, is often the result of caramel coloring in these Californian brandies, but the major reason for their lack of complexity and finesse is that they are made using a Coffey or tower still, which allows a continuous inflow of wine, and increases the volume of the distilled product. This is the system used in the production of gin, vodka and some cheaper blended whiskies.

There is good news, however. A handful of California distilleries, notably those that do not make table wine, employ the alambic still, used by the French to distill cognac. The brandy is made in small batches and the still must be emptied and cleaned after each distillation. In addition, alambic brandies go through two distillations. The biggest problem these producers have is that being relatively new they must wait for several years before their brandy can be released. Good brandy needs years of aging in oak barrels. Nevertheless some remarkably good brandy is being made, the equal of many fine cognacs but with an intensity of fruit unique to California.

Remy-Cointreau of France entered the arena several years ago at Carneros Alambic. Their brandies were very good but they decided to throw in the towel in 2003 and their Napa property was sold to Beringer Blass and re-opened as Etude Wines with not a brandy in sight.

Farther north in central Mendocino County, Hubert

Germain-Robin along with his partner Ainsley Coale established his alambic distillery in 1982. Their brandies, using different varietals of premium wine grapes, have become the benchmark for quality Californian brandies and have been compared to the finest cognac.

Jepson is another well-known Mendocino-based alambic distillery but the property has recently had a change of ownership and has been renamed Jaxon Keys Winery and Distillery. The brandy, made exclusively from French Colombard, the wine traditionally used for cognac, is still marketed under the Jepson label. Because of the necessary long aging process, it will be several years before the distilling skills of the new ownership can be assessed.

The Karakasevic family has been distilling spirits for twelve generations. They moved from Europe to America in 1962 and started distilling in California in 1983. Their **Domaine Charbay** distillery produces a wide range of spirits and even table wines but they bottled their first brandy in 2009. It was distilled in 1983 and promises to be well worth sipping. Prolonged aging is the signature of Domaine Charbay brandy; Miles Karakasevic explains that he wants to make brandy that "you have to eat with a spoon."

The new kid on the block is **Ococalis Distillery** near Santa Cruz, founded in the early 1990s with their first release in 2003. An advantage Californian brandy distillers have over their French counterparts is the large number of grape varieties available to them. Although Osocalis mainly blends from Pinot Noir and Colombard they also use a wide variety of other grapes to give their brandies a distinctive style. They have a close relationship with Santa Cruz Mountain Vineyards and Osocalis brandy is used for their classic port-style fortified wine, the only North American port to be fortified with brandy made with fruit from the same winery.

BRANDY DISTILLERIES

Jaxon Keys
10400 South Highway 101
Hopland, CA 95449
Tel: 707 468 8936
www.jaxonkeys.com
Open daily 10AM–5PM.

Domaine Charbay
4001 Spring Mountain Rd
St Helena, CA 94574
Tel: 707 963 9327
www.charbay.com
Open daily 10AM–4PM
except major holidays.

Osocalis Distillery
5579 Old San José Road
Soquel, CA 95073
Tel: 831 477 1718
www.osocalis.com
Open by appointment
only.

Sake

Sake is the wine of Japan.
It contains alcohol but the
similarities to any other
California wine end there.
First, it is made from rice.
In wine, alcohol is produced
by fermenting sugars found
naturally in grapes. In
sake it is a brewing process
similar to making beer.
Fermentation of rice and
water converts glucose into
alcohol through the work
of enzymes and yeast. The
sake you buy in the store
usually contains around 15
percent alcohol by volume,
not unlike many—some
may say too many—Cali-
fornia wines!

Although only rice and
water are used, the process
is quite complex. The rice

is polished to remove pro-
teins and oils leaving just
starch. The more the rice
is polished, the better the
sake. The rice is allowed to
rest, washed to remove rice
powder and then soaked.
Cooking is the next stage,
which has to be carefully
controlled to prevent over-
or under-cooking, both
of which have an adverse
effect on flavors. The next
process is multiple paral-
lel fermentation. Some of
the cooked rice is injected
with *kōji* mold that converts
starch to glucose. When
the kōji is ready, a starter
mash is made with kōji
rice, water and yeast mixed
together, freshly steamed
rice is added and the
mixture is cultivated for
ten to fifteen days. For the
next three days, the mash
is doubled in quantity each
day by adding more of the
rice-water-kōji mixture.
Staggering the process allows the yeast to keep up
with the increased volume.
Now the main mash is left
to ferment for anything
from two to six weeks. The
longer the fermentation,
the higher the quality of
the sake. After fermenta-
tion, the mixture is pressed
to separate the liquid from
the solids and then filtered

before the final product is pasteurized and left to rest and mature for up to six months before diluting with water to bring the alcohol level down to 15 percent before bottling.

There is a common misconception that sake should be served hot. In Japan sake is served at a temperature to match the season or the food and premium sake is usually served cold to preserve the subtle, delicate flavors that heat destroys. All sake should be consumed as soon as possible after release; freshness is the key. It is not a wine to age. It should be stored in dark, cool conditions and ideally drunk within a few hours of opening. Like wine it can be stored in a refrigerator for a couple of days but once opened it starts to oxidize and the flavor is affected. A rubber wine vacuum top is a good solution.

Northern California has become the center for sake production in North America. There is a plentiful supply of high-quality Yamadanishiki rice from the Central Valley and pure water from the Sierra Nevada Mountains. The northern California climate helps, too.

Sake production has none of the romance of wineries. Rice is trucked in by the sackload and converted to sake in industrial factories. Nevertheless, both seeing the process, and certainly tasting the results, makes for an interesting diversion from the wine-tasting circuit. The only sake house in Napa closed its doors in 2004 but close by are **Gekkeikan Sake** in Folsom, just outside Sacramento and **Takara Sake** in Berkeley. Anyone driving to Napa from San Francisco will pass Takara just off the 580 freeway at University Avenue. They offer several different tasting flights and a sake museum but they don't open until noon.

Ozeki Sake was the first major sake brewer in North America. The 300-year-old Japanese company established their brewery in 1979 in Hollister in California's Central Coast area, two hours' drive south of San Francisco. It may be worth a detour if you are visiting the Central Coast wineries but otherwise Takara is a more convenient location and offers a more interesting visit.

SAKE BREWERIES

**Gekkeikan Sake
(USA), Inc**
1136 Sibley Street
Folsom, CA 95630
Tel: 916 985 3111
www.gekkeikan-sake.com
Open Mon-Fri
10AM–4:30PM.

Takara Sake (USA) Inc
708 Addison Street
Berkeley, CA 94710
Tel: 510 540 8250
www.takarasake.com
Open daily 12PM–6PM.

Ozeki Sake (USA), Inc
249 Hillcrest Road
Hollister, CA 95023
Tel: 831 637 9217
www.ozekisake.com
Open Mon-Fri
8AM–12PM and 1PM–5PM.

**A sake museum at Takara Sake
in Berkeley**

Artisan Foods

California is the breadbasket of the nation but, as with wine, quantity doesn't necessarily equal quality. Until you see the scale of agriculture in California's Central Valley it's hard to imagine just how vast it is. Acre upon acre of crops spread across the valley floor, all produced on an industrial scale and frequently with the help of pesticides and chemical nutrients. Just off Interstate 5 near Coalinga the stench of tens of thousands of cows crowded together on feedlots fills the air for miles. This is about as far as you will ever get from grass-fed beef.

Maybe as a backlash Californians have been in the forefront of the green movement with thousands of artisan producers concentrating on sustainable farming and organic practices that lead the country—particularly in the wine regions.

The artisan cheese revolution was given a kick-start by Laura Chenel in the late 1970s on a small farm in Sebastopol in Sonoma County. The company eventually moved to its present home in the renovated Stornetta Dairy in Carneros. In 2006 it was sold to the Rians Group, a French artisan cheese corporation, but nothing has changed. Every supermarket stocks the mild-flavored **Chenel** cheese. A few miles to the west, Jennifer Bice's family have operated a goat dairy since 1968 and her **Redwood Hill Farm** cheese is as good as it gets. Jennifer may not have the name recognition of Laura Chenel but her cheese speaks for itself; it unapologetically tastes of goat, not a dumbed down version for the mass market.

Even further west, in Sonoma, the Callahan family owns **Bellwether Farms**, started by Cindy Callahan in 1986 when she was already in her fifties. To add to the challenge she decided to specialize in sheep's cheese and with her son Liam, Bellwether Farm cheese has become one of the most celebrated in America.

Cowgirl Creamery was started in 1997 by Sue Conley and Peggy Smith in Point Reyes Station on the Marin County coast. In a few years it has become the standard for organic artisan cows' milk cheese. The company has expanded with a new creamery in Petaluma in neighboring Sonoma County and it is one of the few creameries that encourages visits and gives both tasting and cheese-making classes.

Ig Vella was making artisan cheese in Sonoma town before anyone had even heard of the term. He has been making cheese for seven decades—yes, seven! His Dry Jack is aged for two years and rubbed with olive oil, cocoa and black pepper and is one of the best hard cheeses anywhere. The **Vella Cheese** shop is just around the corner from Sebastiani Winery.

Sonoma County is without question the cheese capital of California if not all North America. Whole books have been written on the subject.

The artisan movement isn't just about cheese. There are several small lot, artisan olive oil producers, particularly in Sonoma County, including **DaVero**, **McEvoy Ranch** and **BR Cohn Winery**. Add bread, fruit, vegetables, lamb, duck, eggs, even sustainable seafood and you have everything you could possibly need for not only the healthiest but the best-tasting meal imaginable.

The best way to experience this cornucopia of healthy, wholesome California produce is to visit one of the many farmers' markets that have proliferated throughout the state. Many are little more than weekly street fairs with a few token farmers thrown in to justify the name but the best are wonderful displays of the best local producers have to offer. Particularly notable are the markets in Healdsburg, St Helena, Santa Rosa, Marin County, Santa Barbara, San Francisco Ferry Building and Salinas.

If you can't find a farmers' market there are an increasing number of stores selling quality produce. The Whole Foods Market chain has stores throughout California and although their nickname "Whole pay check" has some justification—they are not inexpensive—most, not all, their produce is as fresh and organic as you can get outside the farmers' markets. The locavore movement is particularly strong on the West Coast and even giant supermarket chains like Safeway are promoting locally-grown produce. Be careful, however; just because it's local doesn't mean it's fresh—or good!

The locavore movement and belief that organic is always better are ideals that have a sound, commendable basis but beware of the greenwashers. The "green" concept has become so trendy that it sometimes seems that everything is "green" and for many less scrupulous companies the only green they are interested in is the mighty dollar. Look carefully at wording. "All natural" is often used on packaging giving a green implication, but remember that arsenic is all natural too but far from green. The organic section of supermarkets is always the most expensive part of the store, but why should you have to pay a premium for organic mushrooms when all mushrooms are organic? Be careful. Everyone is after your money.

We are fortunate to live in a time when both the quality and range of food has never been better and nowhere do these come together in such profusion as in California's wine country. *Bon Appetit!*

Cowgirl Creamery at Tomales Bay Foods
80 Fourth Street Point Reyes Station, CA 94956
Tel: 415 663 9335
Wed-Sun 10AM–6PM, Friday morning tours at 11:30AM and 3:00PM on select summer days (reservations required).

THE COWGIRL CREAMERY

WEBSITES

Websites relating to California and the wine industry are so numerous that it would take the whole book to list them all. This is a small selection.

www.wineinstitute.org
The leading association of California wineries.

www.visitcalifornia.com
The main tourism website for the state. Provides links to all major tourist areas.

WINE WEBSITES

These are the official sites for the major wine regions:
www.amadorwine.com
www.calaveraswines.org
www.lodiwine.com
www.montereywines.org
www.napavalley.com
www.pasowine.com
www.placerwine.com
www.sbcountywines.com
www.sonomacounty.com
www.sonomavalley.com
www.temeculawines.org
www.truemendocinowine.com
www.wineroad.com

All Sonoma wine country outside of Sonoma Valley is covered on this site.

ACTIVITY WEBSITES

www.winecountry.com
Comprehensive site for all California wine country activities, lodging, food and even real estate.

www.getawayadventures.com
Bike and kayak tours

www.winetrain.com
Napa's dining experience on rails

www.platypustours.com
Wine tours of Napa and Sonoma

www.californiawinehikes.com
Hiking and wine tasting tours

www.beauwinetours.com
Napa limousine tours

www.balloonrides.com
Balloon adventures

www.up-away.com
Napa balloon rides

www.hotairadventures.com
Sonoma balloon rides

WINE EVENTS

JANUARY
**Mendocino Crab
and Wine Days**
Fort Bragg
A festival of wine and
seafood.
www.visitmendocino.com

ZAP Zinfandel Festival
San Francisco
www.zinfandel.org

JANUARY–MARCH
Napa Mustard Festival
Napa Valley
A celebration of Napa Valley's food, wine and culture
at a time of the year when
wild mustard flowers in the
vineyards.
www.mustardfestival.org

MARCH
**Rhone Rangers
Grand Tasting**
San Francisco
A tasting of Rhône-style
wines.
www.rhonerangers.org

**Russian River Barrel
Tasting**
Russian River Wine Road
www.wineroad.com

World of Pinot Noir
Shell Beach
www.worldofpinotnoir.com

APRIL
**Pebble Beach Food
and Wine**
Pebble Beach
www.pebblebeachfoodand-
wine.com

MAY
**Anderson Valley
Pinot Noir Festival**
Boonville, Anderson Valley
www.avwines.com

Hospice du Rhône
Paso Robles
A three-day event, including seminars, meals and
tastings of Rhône grape
varieties.
www.hospicedurhone.org

JUNE
Monterey Wine Festival
Monterey, California
www.montereywine.com

Napa Wine Auction
St Helena, Napa Valley
www.napavintners.com

Pinot Days
Fort Mason, San Francisco
www.pinotdays.com

AUGUST
**Family Winemakers
of California**
Fort Mason, San Francisco
www.familywinemakers.org

**Russian River Valley
Grape to Glass Weekend**
Russian River Wine Road
www.rrvw.org

**SEPTEMBER
Kendall Jackson Heirloom
Tomato Festival**
Santa Rosa
www.kj.com/events/tomato-
festival

**Sonoma Wine
Country Weekend**
Sonoma
www.sonomawinecountry-
weekend.com

Winesong
Mendocino Coast
Botanical Gardens
Annual wine tasting and
charitable auction.
www.winesong.org

**OCTOBER
Amador Vintners Big
Crush Harvest Festival**
Amador County
www.amadorwine.com

**NOVEMBER
Mendocino Wine and
Mushroom Festival**
Mendocino County
www.visitmendocino.com

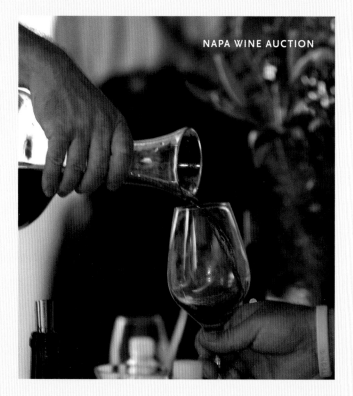

NAPA WINE AUCTION

GRAPE VARIETIES

WHITES

Chardonnay The ubiquitous Burgundian grape of California, now grown everywhere, often because it commands the highest price for white grapes. FLAVOR HINTS: entirely depends upon where the fruit is grown but the underlying flavors are apple and melon, plus butter and toast if the wine goes through malolactic fermentation and aging on oak.

Chenin Blanc Generally grown in the Central Valley for bulk wines. A tiny handful rise above this level of quality. FLAVOR HINTS: honey, quince, minerals.

Gewürztraminer This Alsatian grape grows particularly well in the Anderson Valley and in some of the cooler corners of the Sonoma Coast and Monterey County. FLAVOR HINTS: intense floral nose, roses and lychees.

Muscat Muscat Canalli and Orange Muscat are grown in the Central Valley for dessert wines. The best are very good. FLAVOR HINTS: floral, orange, citrus.

Pinot Gris A fashionable grape, grown with very mixed results in California. The Italian variant, Pinot Grigio, is often thin and one-dimensional in California, but better in Oregon. FLAVOR HINTS: should be honey and spice but is frequently bland and undistinguished.

Riesling The best grapes are grown in the Anderson Valley, Sonoma Coast, Monterey County and, surprisingly, in the Sierra Foothills. Styles vary from sweet to dry. FLAVOR HINTS: depends on the style but generally peaches and green apples.

Sauvignon Blanc Grows throughout the state and is rapidly gaining popularity over Chardonnay. Style varies from New Zealand influenced to a bigger, oaked style. FLAVOR HINTS: grassy, asparagus, grapefruit, melon, passionfruit, depending on style.

Sémillon Very few vines are planted in the state but a handful of wineries introduce botrytis to make a passable dessert wine.
FLAVOR HINTS: honey, butter.

Viognier The growing popularity of this Rhône varietal has led to very mixed results. The best fruit tends to come from Mendocino County and Napa.
FLAVOR HINTS: aromatic flowers and fruit with apricot and peach.

REDS

Barbera A big Italian varietal that grows well in the Sierra Foothills.
FLAVOR HINTS: cherry, plum, spice.

Cabernet Franc Usually grown for Bordeaux blends but a few wineries make an excellent single varietal wine.
FLAVOR HINTS: raspberry, green pepper, blackberry.

Cabernet Sauvignon This noble grape is grown as widely as Chardonnay. Napa is the epicenter of Cab country but the grape grows with considerable success in Sonoma's Alexander Valley, Paso Robles and Sonoma Valley.
FLAVOR HINTS: blackcurrant, black cherry, plum, cedar, cigar box.

Grenache Traditionally this has been grown in the Central Valley for jug wines but a few producers have shown what it can do if planted in the right place.
FLAVOR HINTS: leather, coffee, tobacco, strawberry.

Merlot The grape lost popularity through criticism in the film *Sideways*, but has bounced back. Several excellent Merlots are produced in Napa and some of the cooler regions of Monterey and Sonoma. It is frequently used to blend with Cabernet Sauvignon to soften the tannins.
FLAVOR HINTS: plum, damson, fig, blackcurrant.

Petite Syrah This is a distant relation of Syrah and produces big, inky wines that need long bottle aging.

JORDAN WINERY, ALEXANDER VALLEY

FLAVOR HINTS: savory, dense blackberry, high tannins.

Pinot Noir This great Burgundian grape grows well in the cool coastal regions of California, Carneros, Santa Rita Hills, Sonoma Coast and Anderson Valley. Styles vary widely from huge fruit bombs to elegant, high acid wines.
FLAVOR HINTS: black fruits, raspberry, plum.

Sangiovese Several growers are experimenting with Italian varietals with some success. Piero Antinori was a catalyst for Sangiovese when he opened Atlas Peak Winery in Napa Valley.

FLAVOR HINTS: violets, vanilla, spice.

Syrah This Rhône grape grows throughout California but particularly well in Paso Robles, Santa Barbara County and the Sierra Foothills.
FLAVOR HINTS: violets, blackcurrants, smoke, chocolate.

Zinfandel Zinfandel is always considered a uniquely California grape although its origins go back to the islands of the Adriatic coast. It excels in Dry Creek and the Sierra Foothills.
FLAVOR HINTS: blackberry, raspberry, pepper, raisins, prunes.

FURTHER READING

MAPS AND GUIDES

The American Automobile Association is the best source for maps of California and for specific regions of the state. They have offices throughout California and the maps are free to AAA members and members of overseas affiliates such as the British AA.

Napa-Sonoma Wine Country Map and Guide (Wine Appreciation Guild) — Its four-fold laminated design makes it ideal for traveling.

Silverman, Victor and Glover, Laurie *California (On the Road History)* (Interlink Books, 2012)—A witty, expansive narrative that reveals the real story of the people and places of the Golden State. Included are recommended museums, state parks, and other attractions, alongside literary excerpts from local authors who give readers a sense of California in different eras.

Wolff, Joe and Paperno, Roger *Café Life San Francisco* (Interlink Books, 2012) — This is a superbly photographed guidebook to the city's neighborhood cafés. Highly recommended.

Sinclair, Mick *San Francisco: A Cultural History* (Interlink Books, 2010)—This book offers in depth cultural and historical insights and introduces the visitor to the city's unique present

ACACIA WINERY, CARNEROS

day identity and its links with the past.

Michelin Red Guide to San Francisco Bay Area and Wine Country Restaurants —The definitive restaurant guide for the northern wine country rated by Michelin's well-known star system. Hotels are included.

Zagat San Francisco and Bay Area Restaurants— This well-established series with consumer-generated reviews also covers the wine country.

Reigert, Ray *Hidden San Francisco and Northern California* (Ulysses, 2009)—Covers all of Northern California including accommodations, restaurants and off-the-beaten-path attractions.

BOOKS ON CALIFORNIA WINE COUNTRY

Conaway, James *Napa: The Story of an American Eden* (Mariner Books, 2002)—This social history of Napa Valley is a fascinating glimpse into the world of wealth, power and personalities behind the great winemaking empires.

Deutschman, Alan *A Tale of Two Valleys: Wine, Wealth and the Battle for the Good Life in Napa and Sonoma* (Alan Broadway, 2004)—The title says it all.

Heimoff, Steve *A Wine Journey Along the Russian River* (University of California Press, 2005)—An intimate and engaging tour of one of

Sonoma County's premier wine regions.

Kramer, Matt *Matt Kramer's New California Wine* (Running Press, 2004)—Kramer comprehensively discusses all aspects of the California wine industry with wit and intelligence.

Siler, Julie Flynn *The Rise and Fall of the House of Mondavi* (Gotham Books, 2008)—This saga of the collapse of a dynasty makes a compelling read.

Sullivan, Charles *A Companion to California Wine: Encyclopedia of Wine and Winemaking from the Mission Period to the Present* (University of California Press, 1998)

Taber, George *Judgment of Paris: California vs France and the Historic Paris Tasting that Revolutionized Wine* (Simon & Schuster, 2005)—The story of the competition that put California wines on the world map.

Weiss, Mike *A Very Good Year: The Journey of a California Wine from Vine to Table* (Gotham Books, 2005)—A behind-the-scenes look at the making of a premium California wine.

GENERAL WINE BOOKS

Clarke, Oz *Oz Clarke's Encyclopedia of Grapes* (Harcourt, 2001)—The definitive book on wine grapes.

Holmes, Robert, Andrea Johnson, Jordan McKay *Passion for Pinot* (Ten Speed Press, 2009)—A comprehensive illustrated survey of West Coast Pinot Noir.

Kramer, Matt *Making Sense of Wine* (Running Press, 2004)—An intelligent and beautifully-written book on wine.

McCoy, E *The Emperor of Wine* (HarperCollins, 2005)—A critical biography of Robert Parker, the world's most influential critic.

Reichl, Ruth (Ed.) *History in a Bottle* (Modern Library, 2006)—An anthology of great wine writing.

Robinson, Jancis *The Oxford Companion to Wine* (Oxford University Press, 2006)—The complete reference work on wine.

AA (British Automobile Association), xi, 208

AAA (The American Automobile Association), xi, 208

Acacia Winery, 47

Adelaida Cellars, 120, 132

Alameda, 104-5

Alameda Point Vintners, 105

Alexander Valley, 15, 40, 55, 66-7, 69, 83, 206

Allied Domecq, 157

Alma Rosa Winery, 142, 150, 152

Alsatian, 87, 205

Amador County, xvi, 61, 181, 186-9, 204

Amador Vintner Big Crush Harvest Festival, 204

Anderson Valley, 83, 86-8, 203, 205, 207

Anderson Valley Pinot Noir Festival, 203

Archery Summit, 135

Arista Winery, 56, 72, 79

Arrowood Winery, 56, 63, 76

Arroyo Grande, 133-7, 141

Arroyo Seco, 110

Artesa Winery and Vineyards (Codorniu Napa), 5, 46, 48

Atlas Peak Winery, 207

Au Bon Climat Tasting Room, 150, 152

Auberg du Soleil, 39

AVAs (American Viticultural Areas) xiii, xv-xvi; Napa, 18, 26, 28-29, 35, 42; Sonoma, 55, 65, 74-5; Mendocino, 88, 96-7; San Francisco, 111, 113; Central Coast, 119, 126-8, 130-1, 134; Santa Barbara, 147, 150; Southern California, 162; Central Valley, 174; Sierra Foothills, 186

Baileyana Winery, 120, 135, 137

Baja California, 161

Barbera, 184, 188, 206

Beaulieu Vineyards, 5, 18, 20, 23

Bel Air, 162

Bella Vineyards, 56, 70, 78

Bella Vista Vineyard and Winery, 56, 158, 160, 164

Benziger family, 63-4

Benziger Family Winery, 56, 64, 77

Berghold Estate Winery, 170, 173-4, 178

Beringer Blass, 194

Beringer Brothers, 47

Beringer family, 18, 21, 94

Beringer Vineyards, (Rhine House), 5, 18, 21, 25, 69-70

Berkeley, 197-8

Bernardo Winery, 158, 161, 164

Bernardus Vineyards, 120, 124-5, 127

Bien Nacido, 141

Big Sur, 119, 126

Black Muscat, 176

Black Sheep Vintners, 182, 191

Boeger Winery, 182, 184-5

Bogle Winery, 170, 174, 178

Boisset Family Estates, 18, 72

Boonville, 83, 89, 93, 98-99, 203

Bordeaux, xvi, 7, 16, 21, 29, 36, 96, 162, 185, 206

Bottle Shock, 28

Bouchaine Vineyard, 5, 47-8

BR Cohn Winery, 56, 62, 76, 200

brandy, 22, 91-2, 194-6

Brassfield Estate Winery, 84, 97

Breggo Cellars, 84, 88

Brown Forman Group, 89

Buelton, 154

Buena Vista Winery, xii, 61, 75

Burgundy, xiv, 46, 62, 72, 75, 113, 127, 205, 207

Burrell School Vineyards & Winery, 84, 114-5

Cabernet Franc, xvi, 7, 130-1, 146-7, 185, 206

Cabernet Sauvignon, xiii, xvi, 3, 6-7, 10, 14-15, 17-18, 21-4, 26, 29, 33-6, 39-40, 55, 65-6, 69, 94, 130-1, 146, 188, 206

Cakebread Cellars, 5, 17, 19

Calaveras County, 181, 190-1

Calaveras County Big Trees State Park, 191

Calcareous Vineyard, 120, 129, 132

The Calera Wine Co., 127

California Highway Patrol, xviii, 32

California Republic, 59
California State Fair Commercial Wine Competition, xix
California State Historic Landmark, 186
Calistoga, 3, 6-7, 25-31, 40, 46, 51, 95
Callaway Winery, 157-8, 164
Cambria, 73, 134, 142, 144
Cambria Winery and Vineyard, 144, 151
Camino Real, 59, 119
Campovida (Valley Oaks Center), 89
Cannery Row, 122, 128, 139
Cardinale Winery, 5, 14, 19, 72
Carhartt Vineyard, 142, 147
Carmel, 122-8
Carneros, *see Los Carneros*
Carneros Vineyards, 29
cava, 45
Central Coast, xiii, 40, 119-39, 197
Central Valley, xii-xiii, 101, 169-79, 197, 199, 206
Chablis, xiv
Chalk Hill, 65-66
Chalk Hill Winery, 56, 65, 77, 151
Chalone, 126-7
Chalone Vineyards, 120, 126-7
Chamisal Vineyards, 120, 135, 137
champagne, 28, 36, 46, 87, 169
Chardonnay, xiii, xvi, 3, 7, 10, 14, 25, 28-9, 39, 41, 45-7, 55, 65-7, 69, 71-2, 75, 86, 109, 111-4, 119, 123, 127, 135-7, 141, 145, 150-1, 157, 184-5, 205-6
Charles Krug Winery, 5, 15, 23, 25, 33
Charles M. Schultz Museum, 58, 79
Château Beaucastel, 129
Chateau Bellevue Winery, 110
Château Julian Wine Estate, 120, 125, 227
Chateau Margene, 120, 130, 133
Chateau Montelena, 3, 5, 18, 25-6, 30
Chateau Souvrain, 69
Chateau St. Jean, 56, 65, 77
Chatom Winery, 182, 191
cheese, 199-200

Chenin Blanc, 205
Chimney Rock Winery, 5, 33-4, 40
Christian Brothers, 22, 194
Cinsault, 185
Citizen Kane, 134
Claiborne & Churchill Vintners, 120, 135, 137
Clarksburg, 174, 178
Clautiere Vineyard, 120, 131-3
Clear Lake, 94, 97
Cliff Lede Winery, 5, 35, 41
Cline Cellars, 5, 43-4, 48
Clos du Val, 5, 33, 40
Clos Pagase, 5, 29-30
Coffey (tower still), 194
cognac, 91, 194-5
colombard, 195
Concannon Vineyard, 102, 109, 111
Constellation Brands, 16, 62-3, 144-5, 173, 175
Contra Costa County, 43, 110
Cooks Champagne, 175
Coppola, Francis Ford, 17, 69
Cornell Winery and Tasting Room, 158, 163-5
Cougar Vineyards, 160, 164
Cowgril Creamery (Petaluma, Tomales Bay Foods), 199-201
Crimson Group, 135
The Culinary Institute of America, 22
Cuvaison Winery, 5, 29-30, 46, 48

Da Vero, 200
David Bruce Winery, 114
Darioush Winery, 5, 32, 40
Dehlinger Winery, 56, 78
DeLoach, 19, 56, 72, 79
Diageo, 29, 105
di Rosa, 45, 48
Disney/ Disneyland, x, 6, 150
Dolce, 14
Domaine Carneros (Tattinger), 5, 45-6, 48
Domaine Chandon (Champagne's Moët & Chandon), 5, 11, 13
Domaine Charbay, 195-6
Duckhorn Wine Company (Paraduxx Winery, Duckhorn Vineyards), 5, 35, 39, 41, *see also*

Goldeneye (Duckhorn Winery)
driving, roads, xi, xiv, xvi-xviii, 208
Dry Creek, 55, 69-71, 207

East Paso, 130-3, *see also Paso Robles*
Easton Wines, 188, *see also Terre Rouge*
Eberle Winery, 120, 133
Edmeades Winery, 87
Edna Valley, 133-5
El Dorado County, 181, 184-6
Esterlina Vineyards, 84, 88
Etude Wines (Carneros Alambic), 194

Failla, 5, 39-41
Family Winemakers of California, 203
Far Niente Winery, 5, 14, 15, 19, 89
Ferrari Carano, 56, 69, 78
Fess Parker Winery and Vineyards, 142, 146, 152
festivals, Sonoma, 66, 73; Mendocino, 86; Southern California, 160; Central Valley, 173;
Wine Events, 203-204; *see also wine competitions*
Fetzer family, 89-90
Ficklin Vineyards, 170, 177
Fiddlestix Tasting Room & Winery, 142, 151-2
Firepeak Vineyards, 135
Firestone Vineyard, 142, 146, 152
Flora Springs Winery and Vineyard, 5, 24-5
Foley, Bill, 37, 61, 66, 146, 151
Foley Estates Winery, 142, 151, 153, *see also Foley Vineyards*
Foley Vineyards, 146, *see also Foley Estates Winery*
Folsom, 197-8
food, xvii; Napa, 8, 11, 13, 22-3, 34-5, 39, 45, 49-51; Sonoma, 55, 66, 69-70, 72-3; Mendocino, 98-9; San Francisco, 101, 104, 106, 108, 116-7; Central Coast, 131, 133-4, 138-9; Santa Barbara, 146, 148-150, 154-5; Southern California, 160-1, 166-7; Central Valley, 173, 179, 185; Sierra Foothills, 192;

Beyond Wine, 199-201, 203-4; Further Reading, 208-9
Fort Bragg, 86, 92-3, 203
Fosters, 21
Foxen Winery, 142, 145-6, 152
Francis Ford Coppola Winery, 56, 69, 77
Franciscan Estates, 39
Freemark Abbey, 72, 114
Frog's Leap, 5, 17, 20

Gainey Vineyard, 142, 148, 152
Galante Vineyards, 120, 128
Gallo (E & J Gallo Winery), 110, 169, 172, 194
Gallo of Sonoma, 169
Gary Farrell Vineyards & Winery, 56, 72, 79
Gary Pisoni Winery, 126
gas (petrol), xvii
Gavilan Mountains, 126-7
Gekkeikan Sake, 197-8
General Vallejo home & museum, 61
Germain-Robin, 84, 91, 93, 195
Gewürztraminer, 87, 205
Geyser Peak Winery, 56, 67, 77
gin, 194
Gina Gallo, 110
Glen Ellen, 63-4, 76-7
Gloria Ferrer Caves and Vineyard, 5, 45, 48
Gold Country, 110, 186, 188
Gold Rush, xii, 61, 181, 190
Golden Gate International Exposition, 106
Goldeneye (Duckhorn Winery), 88
Grands Amis Winery, 170, 178
Green Valley, 73-5
Grenache, 185, 206
Greystone Cellars, 22
Grgich Hills Estate, 5, 18, 20
Grgich, Mike, 18, 28
Groth, 5, 17, 19
Guenoc, 97
Guerneville, 81

Hacienda de las Rosas Tasting Room, 158, 161, 165
Hall Wines, 5, 24-5

Handley Cellars, 84, 88, 92
Hanzell Vineyards, 56, 62, 75
Haraszthy, Agoston, xii, 61
Hartford Court, 56, 72, 74, 79
Healdsburg, 66, 77-81, 200
Hearst Castle (Xanadu), 134
Hearst, William Randolph, 134
Heitz Cellars, 5, 23, 25
Heitz, Joe, 23-4
The Hess Collection, 5, 9-10
High Valley, 97
Hollister, 127, 197
Hollywood, 8, 141
Hopland, 89-90, 93, 96, 99
Hospice du Rhône, 203
hotels, xviii
Howell Mountain, xvi
Hudson Vineyards, 45
Husch Vineyards, 84, 87, 92

Imagery, 56, 63, 76-7
insurance, xviii
Iron Horse Vineyards, 56, 74, 79
Ironstone Winery Heritage
    Museum, 182, 190-1

Jack London State Park, 64
Jackson Family Wines, 65
Jackson, Jess, 14, 65, 72, 79, 87
Jacuzzi Family Vineyards (The
    Olive Press), 5, 44-5, 48
Jaxon Keys Winery and Distillery
    (Jepson), 195
Jeriko Estate Winery, 84, 90, 95
Jimtown Store, 69, 79
JLohr, 120, 123, 130, 133
Jordan Winery, 56, 69, 78
The Joy of Cooking, 39
Judgment of Paris, xii, 3, 18, 25, 28,
    34, 210
Justin Vineyards and Winery, 120,
    129, 131-2

Karly Wines, 182, 188, 190
Kendall-Jackson, 14, 55, 72, 94, 144,
    204, see also Jackson Family Wines and
    Kendall Jackson Wine Center
Kendall Jackson Heirloom Tomato
    Festival, 73, 204
Kendall Jackson Wine Center, 56,
    73, 79
Kenneth Volk Winery (Byron
    Winery), 142, 144-5, 151
Korbel, 194
Krug, Charles, 3, 20, 23
Kuleto Estate, 5, 36, 41
Kuleto Winery, 151

L'Aventure Winery, 120, 132
La Jota, 72
La Riconada, 151
La Rochelle/ Steven Kent Winery,
    102, 110-1
Laetitia Vineyard and Winery
    (Maison Duetz), 120, 137
lager, 21
Lake County, 94-6, 106
Lakeport, 99
Landmark Vineyards, 56, 65, 77
Langtry Estate and Vineyards, 84,
    96-7
Las Vegas, 23, 32, 150
Lava Cap Winery, 182, 185
liquor, 91
Livermore, 105, 108-10
Lodi, 108, 172-4, 178-9
The Lodi Grape Festival, 173
Lodi Wine and Visitor Center,
    173, 178
Lompoc, 147, 151-3
Londer Vineyards, 84, 88
London, Jack, 64
Longoria Wines, 142, 147, 151-2
Loring, 151
Los Angeles, xvii, 119, 141, 161-2, 166
Los Angeles County, 161
Los Carneros, 7, 26, 29, 34, 36, 42,
    45-6, 51, 75, 114, 199, 207
Los Gatos, 114-5, 139
Los Olivos, 146, 154-5
Los Olivos Café and Wine
    Merchant, 147
Louis Martini Winery, 169
Luther Burbank's House, 58, 79
Lynmar Estate, 56, 72, 79

Madera, 174-9
Madera Wine Trail, 175
Madroña Vineyards, 182, 185
Magnanimus Wine Group, 89

Malibu, 162-3, 167
Maple Creek Winery, 84, 89, 93
Marin County, 75, 200
Martell, 91
Martha's Vineyard, 23
Martinelli Winery, 72
Matanzas Creek Winery, 56, 64, 72, 77
Maverick Saloon, 149
McEvoy Ranch, 200
Médoc, 3
Melville Winery, 142, 151-3
Mendocino, xiii, 29, 66, 75, 83-99, 194-5, 203-4, 206
Mendocino Brewing Company, 89
Mendocino Coast Botanical Gardens, 86, 93
Mendocino Crab and Wine Days, 203
Mendocineo Wine and Mushroom Festival, 204
Meritage, xvi
Merlot, xvi, 7, 29, 35, 39, 65-6, 72, 130-1, 146-7, 185, 206
methode champenoise, 28, 45, 169
Michael-David Winery and Phillips Farm Fruitstand Café, 170, 173, 178
Millaire Winery, 182, 191
Mission grapes, 188
Mondavi, Robert/ Mondavi Family, 3, 8, 63, 144, 173, 210
Mont LaSalle Cellars, 10
Monterey, 119, 122-6, 128, 139, 203, 205-6
Monterey Wine Festival, 203
Monteviña Winery, 182, 188, 190
Montrachet, 3
Moraga Winery, 162
Mount Eden Vineyards, 102, 113, 115
Mount Harlan, 127
Mount St Helena, 14, 22, 25, 65, 95
Mount Veeder, 14, 29
Mourvèdre, 185
Murder She Wrote, 83
Mumm Napa Valley, 5, 36, 41
Murphys, 190-2
Muscat Canalli, 205
museums, Napa, 8, 11, 13-14, 16, 20, 28-31, 35-6, 44-5; Sonoma, 58, 61, 64, 79; San Francisco, 101; Central Coast, 126; Santa Barbara, 147; Central Valley, 173; Sierra Foothills, 187-8, 190; Beyond Wine, 197; Further Reading, 208

Nadeau Family Vintners, 120, 132
Napa, xii-xiv, xviii, 3-53, 55, 87, 96, 105-6, 114, 119, 131, 135, 151, 160, 162, 169, 172-5, 181, 188, 194, 197, 202-3, 206-9
Napa Mustard Festival, 203
Napa Valley Opera House, 9-10
Napa Wine Auction, 203
National Historic Landmark, 58-59
National Register of Historic Places, 14, 23
National Steinbeck Center, 126, *see also Steinbeck, John*
National Trust for Historic Preservation, 65
Navarro Vineyards, 84, 87, 92
Nevada County, 184
North Coast, 96
Novitiate Winery, 114

Oakville, 13-14, 19, 23, 35, 50
Ocacalis Distillery, 195-6
Old Faithful of California Geyser, 26-8, 30
olive oil, 200
Opolo Vineyards, 120, 131-2
Opus One Winery, 16
Orange Muscat, 176, 205
Oregon, xvii, 83, 110, 135, 205
Ozeki Sake, 197-8

Pacific Star Winery, 84, 86, 92
Paraduxx Winery, *see Duckhorn Wine Company*
Paragon, 135
Parducci Wine Cellars, 84, 90, 92
Parker, Fess, 146-7
Parker, Robert, xviii-xix, 210
Paso Robles, 123, 128-33, 160, 162, 203, 206-7
Paul Masson, 194
Peachy Canyon Winery, 120, 132
Pebble Beach Food and Wine, 203

Peju Province, 5, 17, 19
Petite Syrah, 110, 160, 206
Petite Verdot, 7
phylloxera, xii, 3
Pierce's Disease, 157
Pine Ridge Winery, 5, 34, 40, 135
Pinot Days, 203
Pinot Grigio, 205
Pinot Gris, xvi, 66, 205
Pinot Noir, xvi, 7, 28-9, 34, 36, 40,
    42, 45-7, 55, 65, 71-2, 74-5, 83,
    86-8, 92, 101, 110-4, 119, 123, 126-7,
    130, 135-7, 141, 145, 150-1, 195, 203,
    207, 210
Placerville, 184-5, 192
port, 24, 176-7, 185, 195
Preston Vineyards, 56, 70, 78
Prohibition, xii, 3, 14, 18, 94, 108,
    161, 181, 184

Quady Winery, 170, 175-6, 178
Quintessa, 5, 39, 41

Ravenswood Winery, 56, 61-2, 75
Raymond Vineyards, 5, 18-20
Redwood Valley, 90-2
Renwood Winery, 182, 188, 190
Ridge Vineyards, 102, 113, 115
Riesling, 87, 181, 184, 205
Rhône, xvi, 43, 106, 110, 119, 129,
    157, 185, 187-8, 203, 206-7
Rhone Rangers Grand Tasting, 203
Riverside International Wine
    Competition, xix
roads, driving, xi, xiv, xvi-xviii, 208
Robert Hall Winery, 120, 123
Robert Mondavi Winery, 5, 15-16,
    19, 23, see also Mondavi, Robert/
    Mondavi Family
Robert Renzoni Winery, 160, 164
Robert Sinskey Winery, 5, 34, 40
Rochioli, 56, 71-72, 78
Rock Wall Wines (Rock Wall Wine
    Company), 102, 105-6
Roederer Estate, 84, 87-8, 92
Rombauer Vineyards, 5, 39, 41
rosé, xiv
Rosenblum Cellars, 102, 104-6
Rosenthal, 158, 162, 165
Rousanne, 185

Rubicon Estate (Inglenook Estate),
    5, 17, 20
Rudd Vineyards, 24
Russian River Barrel Tasting, 203
Russian River Valley, xvi, 19, 55, 65,
    71-4, 203-4, 209-10
Russian River Valley Grape to
    Glass Weekend, 203
Rutherford, 13, 17, 19-20, 24, 35-6,
    39, 41, 162
Rutherford Hill Winery, 5, 39, 41

Sacramento, 197
Saintsbury, 5, 46, 48, 114
sake, 196-8
Salinas, 126, 128, 200
San Antonio Winery, 158, 161, 165
San Diego, 161, 164-5
San Diego County, 161, 166
San Francisco, xvii, 3, 42, 55, 95,
    101-17, 119, 128, 197, 203, 208-9
San Francisco 1906 Earthquake,
    58, 101
San Francisco Bay, 44-5, 87, 106, 108
San Francisco Chronicle Wine
    Competition, xix
San Francisco Ferry Building (Ferry
    Building Marketplace, Ferry
    Plaza), 101, 106, 200
San José, 110-3
San Luis Obispo, 119, 131, 134, 137-8
San Pablo Bay, 7, 42, 45-6
San Pasqual Winery, 158, 161, 165
Sanford and Benedict Vineyard, 150
Sanford Winery, 142, 150-2
Sangiovese, xiii, 189, 207
Santa Barbara, xi, 29, 119, 141-55,
    200, 207
Santa Clara, xii
Santa Cruz, 105, 111-5, 119, 139
Santa Cruz Mountain Vineyards,
    195
Santa Lucia Highlands, 123, 126,
    162
Santa Maria Valley, 141, 145-6, 150
Santa Monica, 162
Santa Rita Hills, 119, 146, 150-1, 207
Santa Rosa, 58, 65, 73, 79-80, 200
Santa Ynez Valley, xiii, 141, 145-9
Saratoga, 114-5

Sattui Castle (Castello di Amorosa), 23

Saucelito Canyon Winery, 120, 135, 137

Sauvignon Blanc, 7, 14, 17, 65, 67, 72, 162, 185, 188, 205

Savannah-Chanelle Vineyards (Congress Springs), 102, 114-5

Sbragia, Ed, 22, 56, 69

Sbragia Family Vineyards, 69, 78

Scheid Vineyards, 120, 128

Schramsberg Vineyards, 5, 28, 30

Sea Smoke Cellars, 151

Sebastiani Vineyards and Winery, 56, 61, 76, 151, 200

Sebastopol (Napa), 10-11, *see also Yountville*

Sebastopol (Sonoma), 11, 73, 79, 81, 199

Seghesio Family Vineyards, 56, 66, 77

Sémillon, 7, 14, 206

Serra, Father Junipero, xvii, 119, 133

Sequoia National Park, 175

Shenandoah Valley, 186-8

Shenandoah Valley Museum, 187

Shenandoah Valley Vineyards, 182, 187, 189

Sideways, 119, 141, 145-7, 150, 206

Sierra Foothills, 181-93, 205-7

Sierra Nevada, xi, xiii, 108, 181, 197

Sierra Vista Vineyards, 182, 184-5

Silicon Valley, 110-3

Silver Oak Cellars' Alexander Valley Winery (Lyeth Winery), 56, 67, 77, *see also Silver Oak Winery*

Silver Oak Winery, 5, 19, 29, 67, *see also Silver Oak Cellars*

Silverado Trail, 7, 29, 31-2, 35-6, 39-41, 46, 51

Silverado Vineyards, 34, 40

Simi Winery, 56, 66, 77

Skunk Train (California Western Railroad), 86, 93

Sobon Estate (D'Agostini Winery), 182, 186-9

Solar Living Institute, 90, 93

Soledad, 126-7

solera system, 177

Solvang, 149-51, 155

Somerston Vineyards (Somerston Estate), 5, 11-12, 37-8, 41

Sonoma, xi-xiv, xvii, 14, 19, 29, 39-40, 42, 46, 55-81, 83, 105-6, 119, 151, 172-3, 175, 181, 199-200, 202, 204-9

Sonoma Coast/ TRUE Sonoma Coast, 40, 55, 75, 205, 207

Sonoma State Historic Park, 61

Sonoma Wine Country Weekend, 204

soutirage, 29

South Coast Winery, Resort and Spa, 160

Southern California, 157-67

sparkling wine, 28, 36, 45-6, 75, 137, 169, 175

Spring Mountain Vineyard, 5, 24

Spring Mountain Winery, 21

St Helena, xviii, 6, 9, 20-5, 41, 50-1, 200, 203

St Supéry's, 5, 16, 19

Stags Leap district, 33-4

Stag's Leap Wine Cellars, 3, 5, 34, 40

Steinbeck, John, 122, 126

Sterling Vineyards, 5, 28, 30

Stevenot Winery, 182, 191

Still Waters Vineyards, 133

Stonestreet, 72

Stornetta Dairy (Chenel Cheese), 45, 199

Story Winery, 182, 188-9

Summers Estate Winery, 5, 28, 30

Sutter Home Winery, 21, 174, 188

Syrah, xvi, 7, 65-6, 72, 146-7, 151, 185, 188-9, 206-7

Tablas Creek, 120, 129, 132

Table Wine, xvi, 3, 194

Takara Sake (and sake museum), 197-8

Talbott Vineyards, 120, 123, 127

Talley Vineyards, 120, 136-7

Taste of Lodi, 173

A Taste of Monterey, 120, 128

Tchelistcheff, Andre, 18, 23

telephone, xviii

Temecula, 157, 160-1, 164, 166

Terlato Family Wines, 150

Terre Rouge, 182, 188, 190, *see also Easton Wines*
Testarossa Winery, 102, 114-5
Thomas Coyne Wines, 102, 110-1
Thomas Fogarty Winery, 102, 113-4
Tobin James Cellars, 120, 131, 133
transportation (public), xvii-xviii, 101
Treasure Island, 44, 106
Trefethen Vineyards, 5, 10
Turley Wine Cellars, 40
Turnbull Cellars, 5, 16, 19
Twomey Cellars, 5, 29

V Sattui Winery, 5, 23, 25
Ventana Vineyards, 120, 128
vermouth, 176
Viansa Winery and Italian Marketplace, 5, 42, 48
Vie Winery, 106
Villa C'Toga, 28, 30
Vine Hill Winery, 102, 114-5
Vino Noceto Winery, 182, 189-90
Vino Piazza, 174, 178
Vintage 1870 (Groezinger Winery), 5, 11-12
Viognier, xiii, 7, 146, 185, 206
vodka, 194

Ukiah, 89-91, 93

Wattle Creek, 102, 106
websites, 202
Wells, Orson, 134
Wente Vineyards, 102, 108, 111
West Paso, 128-32, *see also Paso Robles*
Whalebone Vineyard, 120, 129, 132
whiskey, 194
Wild Horse Winery, 120, 133, 144-5
William Hill Winery, 169
Williams Selyem Winery, 56, 78
Windward Vineyard, 120, 130, 132
wine, buying and labels, x, xiv, xviii-xix; Napa, 25, 52-3;

Sonoma, 57; Mendocino, 85; San Francisco, 101; Central Coast, 121; Santa Barbara, 143; Southern California, 159; Central Valley, 171; Sierra Foothills, 183; Wine Events, 203
wine competitions, xix
Wine Garage, 25, 31
wine, sustainable practices, Napa, 17-19, 34, 43, 46; Sonoma, 64, 70, 72; Mendocino, 89-91; Central Coast, 135-6; Santa Barbara, 150-1; Sierra Foothills, 185, 188; Beyond Wine, 199-200
Wine Train, xviii, 9-10
wineries, visiting, xviii-xiv, xvii
The Winery, 102, 106-7
Winery Collective, 102, 107
Winery Lake Vineyard, 45
Wines of Vine Hill, *see Vine Hill Winery*
Winesong, 86, 204
Woodbridge, 170, 173, 178
World of Pinot Noir, 203
The World's Fair, 44
World War II, 106

Yamadanishiki rice, 197
Yerba Buena Island, 106
Yorkville Highlands, 88-9, 93
Yosemite National Park, 175
Yount, George, 10-11
Yountville, 10-13, 34-5, 39, 41, 49-50
Yquem, 14

Zap Zinfandel Festival, 203
ZD Wines, 36, 41
Zinfandel, xvi, 7, 22-3, 26, 35, 40, 43, 55, 61, 66, 69, 72, 104, 106, 113-4, 130-1, 135, 172-3, 181, 184-5, 187-91, 203, 207
Zinfest, 173